100

THINGS TO DO IN
COLUMBUS
BEFORE YOU
DIE

Copyright © 2016 by Reedy Press, LLC
Reedy Press
PO Box 5131
St. Louis, MO 63139, USA
www.reedypress.com

Library of Congress Control Number: 2015954886

ISBN: 9781681060248

Design by Jill Halpin

Cover Image: Jackie Mantey

Printed in the United States of America
16 17 18 19 20   5 4 3 2 1

Please note that websites, phone numbers, addresses, and company names are subject to change or cancellation. We did our best to relay the most accurate information available, but due to circumstances beyond our control, please do not hold us liable for misinformation. When exploring new destinations, please do your homework before you go.

100

THINGS TO DO IN
COLUMBUS
BEFORE YOU
DIE

• • • • • • • • • • • • • • • • • • • •

JACKIE MANTEY

REEDY PRESS

DEDICATION

This book is dedicated to everyone who believes in this town.

CONTENTS

• •

• •

PREFACE

When I graduated from Kent State University in 2008, I decided I wanted to live in one of two places—Pittsburgh or Columbus. Where I ended up depended on who offered me a job first.

Ah, to be young and so willing to leave your entire life up to chance.

Opportunity in Columbus knocked first and I packed my dorm room to head for Ohio's capital city.

I was familiar with Columbus. I grew up an hour north of here in a small town, but visiting with friends had been on the parentally instituted no-fly zone until I was eighteen. So, I was particularly excited to be close to my family and newborn nephew while also having the ability to discover a city that was home to more than eight hundred thousand interesting people.

What I've experienced living here in the last seven years has been nothing short of incredible. I'm sure you're awesome too, Pittsburgh, but I am certainly not sad about where I landed.

Mirroring my personal growth in this town has been the accolades the city has earned since I started my career as a journalist.

In the latest census data, Columbus was the fifteenth fastest growing city in the States and the only one in the Midwest to show a steady uptick in population between 2012 and 2013.

Much of that growth can be attributed to the numerous higher education institutions that call central Ohio home, the mainstay of which is the Ohio State University. A think tank called the Intelligent Community Forum even tapped Columbus as its 2015 Most Intelligent Community in the world, citing its "revolutionary community" approach to new ideas.

Perhaps revolutionary in larger cities, that community approach comes naturally to Columbus. As many longtime residents will attest, this metropolis's scene offers the perfect mix of small town supportiveness and big, worldly ideas, resources, and education. Live here and you can't walk down the street without seeing someone you know and, on the same block, watch a live concert from a nationally touring act or eat at a place Oprah loves.

It was difficult to choose only 100 awesome things to do in this city, but here's a list that covers everything from our favorite traditions to our quirky new interests. Wherever you go, I hope you have fun and come back soon—we'll still be growing!

Jackie Mantey

FOOD AND DRINK

EAT AND SHOP LOCAL
AT THE NORTH MARKET

Love farmers' markets? Here's a place inspired by that one-stop-shop setup that highlights Ohio's culinary and agricultural bounty. Open year-round, the North Market is inside a two-story brick-and-metalwork building that offers a marketplace of produce, flowers, baked goods, cookware, beer, and more. If eating is on the to-do list and not so much grocery shopping, don't miss one of the many prepared food places. Nida's Sushi has a loyal pad thai following. Hot Chicken Takeover, with its battered and fried deliciousness and range of hot sauces, is the current darling of the Columbus food scene. Or chow down on a farm-raised brat from Best of the Wurst. The North Market offers several food, coffee, and wine festivals throughout the year, and in the summer a popular movie series in its parking lot proves Columbus loves this place for more than the amazing things it does for their taste buds.

North Market
59 Spruce St. in the Arena District across from the
Columbus Convention Center, 614-463-9664
www.northmarket.com

TIP

There's plenty nearby to plan a whole day around a North Market visit. Get the food to go and set up a picnic at the neighboring Goodale Park, then cross Park Street to see the incomparable modern art collection at the Pizzuti Gallery. Just be sure to check the gallery's hours first as it's only open to the public during select times.

CLOSE THINGS DOWN
WITH A PEPPERONI NIGHTCAP

Mikey's Late Night Slice has been charming the pants off all of Columbus since opening its Short North pizza place in 2009. The walk-up stand serves thin crust slices of pie slathered in sauce and a smorgasbord of toppings. It's a delicious solve for a late-night case of the munchies. Part of what makes eating here so fun is that when it's not snowing, it screens old cartoons, TV shows, and movies on the brick building next door. Hungry customers can watch as they wait in line or eat outside.

Late Night Slice
1030 N High St. on the east side of the Short North, 614-737-3488
latenightslice.com

TIP
During the warmer months, instead of hailing a cab or an Uber, flag down those people on bikes with a lit-up cart attached. Columbus Pedicab is a bike taxi service that operates in the Short North. Your chariot awaits!

HAVE A FAMOUS
CREAM PUFF

Schmidt's restaurant in German Village is a Columbus culinary landmark. Part of that is because it has been around forever, founded by German immigrants in the 1880s as a meatpacking house and transformed into a restaurant in the 1960s. The other reason for its success? The spot offers delicious, tried-and-true German recipes. It is most beloved for its Bahama Mama sausages and overflowing cream puffs. The sausage is a mixture of beef, pork, and a blend of spices that's an envious family secret; hickory-smoked and served in old-world natural casing links, it's the star of an entrée worthy of the old country. For dessert, try a jumbo cream puff: a flaky, golden-brown baked pastry shell stuffed with a mountain of silky vanilla cream. The restaurant serves hundreds of these half-pound beauties every day, and they're a go-to treat when celebrities or dignitaries visit the Ohio capital. Live music on certain evenings by accordion players in lederhosen provides diners a chance for working off those delicious calories with a jig around the band.

Schmidt's Sausage Haus
240 E Kossuth St., 614-444-6808
schmidthaus.com

SIP CHAMPAGNE
WITH A GRILLED CHEESE

Try a trashy meets classy pairing of Roquefort grilled cheese and a bottle of Dom Perignon at the Blue Danube, just north of campus. The diner-esque Dube, as it's affectionately referred, is a bastion of all-day breakfast frequented by hungover college kids and hungry travelers alike. It's rare to find anything on the menu that's too pricey, so the grilled cheese and champagne offering is a fun exception. With the bottle of Dom, the double sandwich dish is $195, but a $50 version with a bottle of Chandon is available as well. While sipping the bubbly, check out the restaurant's decorative ceiling tiles. Patrons can purchase a tile and decorate it, so the artwork is constantly changing and full of Columbus personality.

The Blue Danube
2439 N High St., just north of the Ohio State University campus
614-261-9308

TIP
Another favorite breakfast spot resides near the Dube. Jack and Benny's (2563 N High St.) is a fuss-free spot to get eggs and all the other a.m. fixings.

BOOZE UP A SLUSHY
AT ODDFELLOWS LIQUOR BAR

This charming wannabe dive bar in the Short North always has a diverse crowd and chill attitude. The oaky decor and fun neon signage have an inviting vibe that's especially attractive in the summer when its large windows are open and the arts district's people watching is at its most entertaining. If it's hot outside, belly up to the sleek wooden bar and order a Lushie. The cleverly named drink is a slushy with liquor added, like the mai tai, a blend of Appleton rum, orange curaçao, pineapple juice, and amaretto. Throughout the week the bar hosts a sweet happy hour too. Trivia nights and PB&J parties, with discounts on Pabst Blue Ribbon beer and a shot of Jameson, abound.

Oddfellows Liquor Bar
1038 N High St., beside Mikey's Late Night Slice, 614-923-9631
oddfellowsliqorbar.com

CELEBRATE THE SEASON
WITH A BUNCH OF NUTS

Strawberry season, that is! Krema Nut Company is one of the oldest peanut butter manufacturing sites in the States. Its facility on a less-traveled road between Grandview and Harrison West sells chocolates, gourmet nuts, and the best smoked almond butter and apple fruit spread sandwich this side of I-270. The nutty goodness is especially decadent in the Classic Old Timer, a sandwich composed of a thick layer of crunchy peanut butter, strawberry preserves, and perfectly sliced fresh strawberries. It's a delicious snack made even yummier when washed down with a Hot & Spicy Peanut Butter Milkshake. Get the sandwiches and milkshakes to go, then head west a few minutes on Goodale Boulevard to C. Ray Buck Park to eat al fresco at a picnic table.

Krema Nut Company
1000 Goodale Blvd., 614-299-4131
krema.com

TASTE PARIS
IN GERMAN VILLAGE

Pistacia Vera is a hopping little pastry shop located along German Village's brick-lined streets. While it sells myriad sweet stuff, its most sought-after items are the Parisian macarons. These colorful little treats are at once chewy and crunchy, made of a light nut meringue cookie with buttercream, ganache, preserves, or curd. With flavors like lavender honey, mocha hazelnut, and raspberry chambord, picking a favorite is deliciously difficult but well worth the effort. The handcrafted delicacies and supporting cast of cinnamon rolls, croissants, and quiche make for a wonderful brunch with a hot cup of coffee inside the cafe or on the sloping patio with a lovely view of German Village. Going to a party? Get a box of these for the host or hostess and be officially crowned best guest ever.

Pistacia Vera
541 S Third St. in German Village, 614-220-9070
pistaciavera.com

TIP
If cupcakes are more likely to register on your sweet tooth cravings list, head a block north on Third St. to Kittie's Cakes. The mini confections are made fresh daily. Must-try flavors include cookies and cream and peanut butter and jelly, which has a red raspberry jelly center.

BE A RETRO
CARNIVORE

Open since the steakhouse heydays of the mid-1950s, the Top still evokes supper club coolness, with its James Dean lighting, wood-paneled dining room, and copper bar. The Top has seen it all—just ask the myriad regulars who shuffle in for a martini—but much to our benefit, they still serve the classics. Charbroiled steaks topped with deep fried onion rings, jumbo lobster tails swimming in juicy butter sauce, and pretty much any cocktail Don Draper and company ever ordered on *Mad Men*. Slide into a massive leather booth and indulge in old-school meat making at its finest. Every night after 6 p.m. a musician creates an auditory ambiance befitting a movie—or AMC TV show—scene.

The Top
2891 E Main St., 614-231-8238
thetopsteakhouse.com

TIP
There's no particular dress code at the Top, but sipping gin martinis around a white tablecloth is much more fun when you're dressed up a little.

EXPLORE
ETHNIC EATS

The taste buds can travel the world during the Columbus Food Adventures's Alt Eats tour. The tour group plans culinary adventures around themes such as taco trucks, coffee joints, and neighborhoods' best and most unique food stops. There are itineraries divided by meal, like a breakfast, brunch, and dessert tour, and itineraries divided by transportation, like a Short North walking tour that hits this hot area of High Street for a fine food crawl. Visitors on the Alt Eats bus tour will experience a diverse menu of food that represents Columbus's vibrant and growing immigrant community. Visits to Somali, Vietnamese, Nigerian, Mexican, and Southern Indian restaurants and cafes along Cleveland Avenue with a bona fide Columbus foodie hosting is as eye opening as it is tasty.

Columbus Food Adventures
columbusfoodadventures.com

TIP
Vegetarians can get in on the Alt Eats action! Just alert the Columbus Food Adventures staff when signing up for the tour. Buy the tickets beforehand so there's a guaranteed seat.

COOL OFF
WITH A SWEET TREAT

Ohio is home to many dairy farms, so it's apropos that central Ohio boasts several outstanding ice cream makers with scoop shops nearby. Try Whit's creamy frozen custard. Jeni's artisanal ice creams have become a national hit—even Oprah gets her Jeni's on. Mix the salty caramel (so beloved, a local band is named after this flavor!) and the hot cayenne chocolate. Graeter's, which has an amazing chocolate chip raspberry ice cream, offers tours of its facilities, and Johnson's Real Ice Cream, with a killer amaretto cherry recipe, has a party room where visitors can see into the space where its ice cream is made. Careful though. Any of these locations will have you screaming for more!

Whit's Frozen Custard
841 N High St. in the Short North, 614-291-9448
whitscustard.com

Jeni's Splendid Ice Creams
714 N High St. in the Short North/various locations, 614-294-5364
jenis.com

Graeter's
Various locations
graeters.com/neighborhood-locations

Johnson's Real Ice Cream scoop shop
2728 E Main St. in Bexley, 614-231-0014
johnsonsrealicecream.com

TRY A CRAFT
DRAFT SODA

Refreshing homemade soda is available at Rambling House, a quaint live music venue in Clintonville. More than four pounds of fresh ginger go into the ginger beer, which is lip-smacking in a mule cocktail. A secret blend of spices goes into the sarsaparilla root beer that tastes like the old-timey good stuff. Interesting carbonated cola combinations include lime grape, blueberry vanilla, and strawberry. While the local soda makers' sugary stuff can also be found at area restaurants and bars, a visit to the whimsical brick-and-mortar location is a must; after all, Rambling House was named after the Irish phrase for a place where the members of a close-knit community meet to catch up on the latest town stories, play music, and clink a glass or two.

Rambling House Soda in Clintonville
310 E Hudson St., 614-468-3415
theramblinghouse.com

TIP
During the evenings when live musicians are entertaining, bring $5 for the cover. All the proceeds from the door go to support the performers. There's no cover on Wednesdays and Sundays.

TAKE
THE THURMANATOR CHALLENGE

Few spots in Columbus can claim the title "As Seen on the Food Network," but Thurman Cafe is one of them. The host of food-challenge show *Man v. Food* tried to eat the Thurmanator in one sitting. It has a well-earned reputation as the baddest burger in the land. This behemoth consists of the following: bun, mayo, lettuce, tomato, pickle, banana peppers, a twelve-ounce burger, bacon, cheddar, another twelve-ounce burger, sautéed mushrooms and onions, ham, mozzarella and American cheese, fries, and a pickle spear (because duh). Eat the whole thing in one sitting and earn Thurman Cafe bragging rights forever. No, really, finishers of this culinary feat could boast for years to come, considering that the restaurant has been a favorite of the Columbus community since 1942.

Thurman Cafe
183 Thurman Ave. (two blocks south of Schiller Park), 614-443-1570
thethurmancafe.com

TIP
Meat and bread lovers should also look into the close-by Katzinger's Delicatessen (475 S Third Street). Made from scratch, Katzinger's sandwiches have a loyal following. Try the sky-high Reuben and don't forget to grab a ginormous pickle from the barrel.

EAT
A PANCAKE BALL

Never heard of a pancake ball? Welcome to Columbus, friends. Katalina's is a top-rated counter-service restaurant in the tree-lined Harrison West neighborhood, a few blocks west of the Short North. Adored for its organic and mostly local food, sprawling outdoor patio, and heaping helpings, Katalina's is most famous for its warm, crunchy-then-creamy pancake balls. These spherical drops of food heaven are made of local stone-ground flour and filled with Nutella, dulce de leche, or pumpkin-apple butter, depending on the season. Ohio maple syrup tops it all off. The menu's oddball extras like sugar and spice bacon or avocado toast further Katalina's rep as a foodie favorite. While it's perfect for brunch, the restaurant has a robust lunch menu as well.

Katalina's
1105 Pennsylvania Ave., near Zeno's bar, 614-294-2233
katalinascolumbus.com

TIP
The line here gets long, so beat the morning rush and come early. Want to wait for the line to go down? Grab a coffee and some free Wi-Fi at the neighboring Caffe Apropos.

HAVE THE BEST VIEW
AT DINNERTIME

Take in the Columbus skyline, Bicentennial Park, and the Scioto Mile at Milestone 229. This restaurant is located downtown along the Scioto River's east bank. Open windows and an impressive patio combine for a view rivaled only by the fresh comfort food. Although it's a hotspot for traveling politicians and people in town for a convention or statehouse visit, Milestone 229 also has a kid's menu so the little ones can enjoy the experience too. After brunch or dinner, walk along the river's beaux arts–style Promenade and Prow. It's stone-paved and lined with trees, flowers, geese, and canopy-covered swings that take everything from date night to a day out with the family up a notch.

Milestone 229
229 S Civic Center Drive, 614-427-0276
milestone229.com

TIP
Plan a visit to Milestone 229 around a live performance at the Columbus Commons. Within walking distance, the Commons is an open green space just south of the Ohio Statehouse with a giant stage that hosts national acts for free throughout the summer.

SPLIT
A LOCAL DRINK AND PIE

Pizza, being a national sport and all, is played exceptionally well in Columbus. Two standout spots for a slice of pie and craft brew, cocktail, or soda are Yellow Brick Pizza in Olde Towne East and Harvest Pizzeria in German Village. Yellow Brick features doughy greasy goodness with a side of quirky humor. With happy hour specials with names like Twin Peaks Tuesday and pizzas with titles like Purple Rain (spicy just like Prince), this is the hip crowd's go-to pizza spot, but anyone with a craving for perfect pizza should hit it up. Harvest has locations in Clintonville and German Village, both with freshly creative pizzas and souped-up sides. The German Village locale is where to go if a craft cocktail is also on the must-have list. Curio is connected to Harvest and has the best signature cocktails in town and an atmosphere that beautifully balances swank and accessibility.

Yellow Brick
892 Oak St. in Olde Towne East, 614-725-5482
yellowbrickpizza.com

Harvest Pizzeria
491 S Fourth St. in German Village, 614-824-1769
harvestpizzeria.com

LEVEL UP
YOUR NIGHTLIFE

The game is on in these bars! And by game we mean Mortal Kombat, Street Fighter, and a competitive round of chess. Since 16-Bit Bar and Arcade opened downtown a few years ago, bars with free arcade games have been popping up like whac-a-moles. 16-Bit features super-fun cocktails named after cinematic cult cultural icons like Dolph Lundgren, Kevin Bacon, and Macho Man Randy Savage, who hailed from Columbus. "Oh yeah!" The nostalgia continues in Clintonville at the Old North Arcade and at the Level One Bar + Arcade in the Crosswoods shopping area north of Worthington. Or go for a round of mini bowling at Woodland's Backyard bar in Grandview. If parlor games are more your style, check out Kingmakers in the Short North. More than five hundred titles line its board game library, making for a wonderful way to whittle the day away with a beer or glass of wine.

16-Bit Bar and Arcade
254 S Fourth St. (downtown), 614-222-1616
16-bitbar.com

Old North Arcade
2591 N High St. in Clintonville, 614-598-0821

Level One Bar + Arcade
130 Hutchinson Ave.
in Crosswoods, just north of the north I-270 on-ramp
level1bar.com

Woodland's Backyard
668 Grandview Avenue, 614-488-2114
woodlandsbackyard.com

Kingmakers
17 Buttles Avenue
on the ground level near Forno, 614-223-1358
kingmakerscolumbus.com

HAVE A HAPPY HOUR
IN A PHOTO BOOTH

The best part about a visit to Club 185, a neighborhood bar that's been slinging suds and good times since 1954, isn't its eclectic crowd, although the mix of young professionals, locals, and lawyers coming home from work or stopping in for happy hour before heading back to the 'burbs always makes for an entertaining experience. The best part isn't the Charles burger served with a fried egg and cheese on Texas toast or icy cold taps of beer or the swallow-you-up booths and vintage decor. The best part? That's the retro photo booth in the corner of this jukebox-pumping, dimly lit spot. Step on in, close the curtain and say cheese. Club 185 makes it easy to create a night to remember.

Club 185
185 E Livingston Ave. in German Village,
just south of downtown, 614-228-3904
club185.com

TIP
This is a great spot for late-night cravings. Club 185 serves food until 1 a.m. and drinks 'til 2:30. Have fun!

DO THE DOG
DOWNTOWN

Have fun with food at Dirty Franks Hot Dog Palace downtown. No where else inside the outer belt can one get a better hot dog cut to look like an octopus over gooey mac and cheese. Quick service and humorous pop art on the walls complement the menu of creative hot dogs, like the Zippity Zam topped in sriracha cream cheese and peppers with a heap of tater tots on the side. For dessert, try the Glad Annie's Old World Baklava, homemade in Worthington with fresh Ohio honey and Amish butter. Add a scoop of Jeni's vanilla bean ice cream and the rest of the dog day will feel dreamy.

Dirty Franks Hot Dog Palace
248 S Fourth St., 614-824-4673
dirtyfrankscolumbus.com

TIP
Got a vegan or vegetarian in the crew? Dirty Franks has plenty of meat-free options that are just as yummy as the all-beef bad boys.

GET AUTHENTIC
JAPANESE FOOD

No frills here. Just incredible food prepared by renowned chef Ryuki "Mike" Kimura. Located in a strip mall, it's a hidden dining gem that locals know about and have frequented for decades. The precise, authentic, and experimental Japanese fare was impressive enough to get a feature spot on Anthony Bourdain's discerning *No Reservations* TV show and it regularly tops lists of the best restaurants in Columbus. With ever-changing menu items like fermented squid, yuzu-infused sauces, stuffed shiitake with shrimp, octopus with vinegar sauce, and barbecued eel, a stop into Kihachi will always garner a dish worth Instagramming. The minimalist ambiance lets diners focus on the unique ethnic blend of flavors.

Kihachi
2667 Federated Blvd. in Sawmill Plaza, 614-764-9040

TIP
Though a diamond in a strip mall's rough, make reservations for a weekend visit.

SUSHI AND SAKE
AT SUNSET

The Short North Arts District has no shortage of wonderful patios, but the wooden and wildlife oasis at Haiku is hands down the best. Slats above the structure allow for just the right amount of shade as greenery and flowers dangle from the open ceiling. A fountain surrounded by tables and chairs creates a Zen-worthy hum. A large curved booth on the outdoor patio that can seat large parties offers fun floor-level seating and the best seat outside the house. Any seat on the patio is a sublime setting for enjoying the freshly prepared sushi, pad thai, and flavorful, seasonal sake. Food is art here and so is the atmosphere. Colder outside? The open kitchen, romantic lighting, and local artwork on the walls inside are just as calming.

Haiku Poetic Food and Art
800 N High St. in the Short North, 614-294-8168
haikucolumbus.com

TASTE FRESH GINGER ALE
AT NORTHSTAR CAFE

For fast and healthy, head to one of this local staple's three locations. The counter-service spots have full outdoor patios and lots of indoor seating, or place an order and pick it up to go; its veggie burgers and iced mint coffee are always great choices for a spring picnic in the Short North's nearby Goodale Park or the Park of Roses if ordering from the Clintonville location. A minimalist urban decor complements the lineup of menu items that don't mess with unnecessary extras, just genuinely fresh ingredients. To experience that commitment to flavor, look no further than the fresh ginger ale. A refreshing blend of ginger, organic cane sugar, lime juice, and mint, it's the type of sweet nectar that garners repeat visitors. The local business also recently opened a new concept in the Short North called Brassica; this is a casual healthy food stop that's open later than many Short North quick dining spots (around 10 p.m.) and makes its food from scratch behind the open counter.

951 N High St. in the Short North
614-298-9999, thenorthstarcafe.com

4241 N High St. in Beechwood between Clintonville and Worthington
614-784-2233

4015 Townsfair Way in Easton Town Center
614-532-5444

TIP

Northstar is also a favorite for locals to grab a cup of coffee or craft beer and work for hours on the free Wi-Fi. Need to spend some time answering emails or just kicking it alone with some caffeine? Northstar's the spot.

DINE AL FRESCO
WITH THE FOODIES

Regularly recognized for its superb American bistro fare, Lindey's in German Village is recognized even more for its lush patio. At brunch, it's divine. Lovely at lunch. Romantic at dinner. Shady white umbrellas dotting the brick ground and gorgeous greenery make it feel at once private and open. The lively setting offers an urban-outdoor ambiance that pairs with everything from the lemon ricotta pancakes to the Ohio Amish chicken. The fancy facade and elegant food need not deter diners from bringing along the kids. Lindey's has a children's menu that's as fun and fresh as the one for adults. Inside, red leather booths and a smooth wooden bar make eating and drinking in this tastefully decorated space just as enjoyable when the weather's not as nice.

Lindey's
169 E Beck St. in German Village, 614-228-4343
lindeys.com

GET FINER
WITH TIME

Sample the best vino at House Wine in Worthington. This local spot serves a well-curated lineup of vintages by the glass or bottle, but the fun standout is its Enomatic wine dispenser. This machine is similar to a fountain pop machine, but better because, well, it's serving twenty-four unique wines that the well-educated staff is happy to elaborate on. It's a delicious way to sample selections that may become a new favorite or to hang out with friends in the cool sitting space. Not a wine drinker? House Wine doesn't discriminate against its spirits: a well-rounded fridge of craft beers is available too.

House Wine
644 High St. in Worthington by Graeter's, 614-846-9463
housewine.biz

TIP
Go during happy hour from 2 to 6 p.m., Monday through Friday, for $10 worth of pours at the Enomatic machine and a complimentary cheese plate.

TASTE-TEST
ALL THE FOOD TRUCKS

A three-day roundup of more than seventy of the best food trucks in Ohio, the Columbus Food Truck Festival is a growing annual festival held every mid-August in the Columbus Commons downtown. In addition to trying the state's innovative cuisine on the go, visitors can listen to live music and entertainment or peruse the goods of various Columbus makers and artists who have set up shop while the kids spend some time at the craft tables. From steamed bagel sandwiches to Jamaican grilled meats, the tummy is bound to find a treat—or five. There's plenty of public parking around this downtown green space and the garage below the statehouse is a safe and close option for stowing away your ride as you stuff yourself with the best tacos and tortillas around.

Columbus Food Truck Festival
columbusfoodtruckfest.com

TIP
Visit the website before the event to print a map of where each truck will be located.

FINE DINING
AT ITS FINEST

The Columbus culinary landscape is a smorgasbord of deliciousness. From Slow Food Columbus's revival of traditional cuisine to the Commissary's rentable kitchen space and classes, the city is a burgeoning beacon of Midwestern food innovation. Three tasty destinations to plug into the GPS as soon as hunger hits include Alana's Food and Wine, which has a daily rotating menu of locally sourced modern dishes by Chef Alana Shock; M at Miranova, a beautifully modern space in a downtown office and condo complex that serves a killer martini and contemporary cuisine; and the Refectory, a renovated church that serves exceptional French food crafted by Chef Richard Blondin, a native of France, and has a wine cellar with more than seven hundred titles.

Alana's Food and Wine
2333 N High St., 614-294-6783
alanas.com

M at Miranova
2 Miranova Place, 614-629-0000
matmiranova.com

Refectory Restaurant and Bistro
1092 Bethel Road, 614-451-9774
refectory.com

IMBIBE A LOCAL BREW

Columbus is the little brewery town that could! Experts in the world of hops abound in the Ohio state capital, much to the benefit of everyone age twenty-one and up. In addition to a robust collection of breweries, the city hosts an annual Summer Beer Fest at the LC Pavilion (columbusbeerfest.com). A tour group called Columbus Brew Adventures (columbusbrewadventures. com) hosts visits to these many beer havens, themed by neighborhoods, like the Brewery District and Grandview, or perfect pairings, like the Pitchers and Pizza tours on various Saturdays. Many of these breweries also have bars and patios ready for enjoying their impressively crafted and comprehensive beers any day of the week. Hit up each site's Facebook page the day of a journey out to taste their suds, as many have food trucks or local entertainment that pop up throughout the week.

Wolf's Ridge Brewing
215 N Fourth St. (downtown), 614-429-3936
wolfsridgebrewing.com

Gordon Biersch
401 N Front St., in the Arena District, 614-246-2900
gordonbiersch.com

Zauber Brewing
909 W Fifth Ave., in Grandview, 614-456-7074
zbeers.com

Actual Brewing Company
655 N James Rd., on the east side, 614-636-3825
(open evenings, Wed-Sat)
actualbrewing.com

North High Brewing
1288 N High St., just north of the Short North, 614-407-5278
northhighbrewing.com

Seventh Son Brewing Co.
1101 N Fourth St., 614-421-2337
seventhsonbrewing.com

ARTS AND ENTERTAINMENT

GO TO AN ARTS FESTIVAL

Celebrate Columbus's growing and vibrant arts community at Independents' Day. This weekend-long outdoor festival held every September is a showcase of indie film, comedy, dance, and aerial performances, street art, craft vendors, food trucks, and live music all day long. It's held in Franklinton, a neighborhood that local artists and entrepreneurs have worked hard to revitalize in the past ten years, surrounding 400 West Rich, the steeple of success in turning this community into a haven for hundreds of artists who have studios in the huge historical building. Independents' Day is the premier way to see Columbus's best artists and musicians all in one weekend. As they say, come for the unprecedented entertainment, stay for the chocolate fountain or whatever fabulously weird entertainment is on the bill.

The Columbus Arts Festival is another weekend-long celebration of visual and musical arts held downtown on the riverfront every June. The Columbus culturati are in attendance alongside hundreds of artists from across the US. Stroll along the banks to find a new masterpiece, make your own art, sample the best food trucks, or see a live band. The all-ages-friendly Columbus Arts Festival was voted as one of the top twenty-five festivals in the country by *Sunshine Artist* magazine.

Independents' Day
thisisindependents.com

Columbus Arts Festival
columbusartsfestival.org

SEE THE LARGEST
FIREWORKS DISPLAY IN THE STATE

Being the state's capital, Columbus's Independence Day celebration has some pressure to represent. Boy, does it. More than four hundred thousand people pile into downtown on July 3 for festivities that begin at noon. A patriotic parade of Uncle Sams, flag twirlers, and fun floats takes place on Main, Front, and Spring Streets while several stages of entertainment dot the downtown area including Bicentennial Park and near Nationwide Arena. The day culminates with an explosive half-hour-long fireworks display that dazzles and delights while a soundtrack of modern and old-time music plays. Proud to be an American? Brave the crowds and find the best views in Bicentennial Park along Long Street, Nationwide Boulevard, Washington Boulevard, and Civic Center. Pop open a chair and a cooler and get ready to celebrate.

Red, White and Boom!
July 3, Downtown
redwhiteandboom.org

TIP
If going downtown to watch seems too daunting (it's packed and, thus, best to arrive early!), try going to Berliner Park to set up a viewing spot. The park is located southwest of downtown at 325 Greenlawn Ave.

WALK
IN THE DOO DAH PARADE

This Fourth of July parade has become notorious for its irreverent, politically incorrect take on America. A lovable skewering of politics and Columbus culture alike have made the Doo Dah Parade a local favorite, and the best part is, of course, that anyone can march in it. Just line up the day of and walk the loop, which starts on Buttles in the Short North, heads up Neil, cuts across Second, and spits out down High. No advertising, no nudity, just good clean rabble-rousing fun. Watching the revelry is equally fun, and the party starts on the streets about an hour beforehand while a stage of live music and, of course, a protest or two, gets things started even earlier on the corner of Buttles and High Streets. Doo Dah is a spirited send-off to the summer holiday and a celebration of the city's prideful progressiveness and social awareness.

July 4, Short North
doodahparade.com

DRINK WINE
WHILE WATCHING A SHOW

Columbus Civic Theater is located in the good-natured, granola-y neighborhood of Clintonville. Its venue is a small renovated building that maintains the architecture of its former life as an old gas station or auto parts store (there are a lot of these kinds of buildings on this strip of Indianola Avenue, a fun drive in and of itself). Columbus Civic Theater produces classic theatrical staples like *Who's Afraid of Virginia Woolff* and Tennessee Williams's *Suddenly, Last Summer*. Upon entry to most plays, visitors are greeted with the offer of cookies or coffee. Patrons can also bring their own wine to drink during the intimate show. (No beer though; it can stain the carpet!) Hit up the local Weiland's Market a few blocks away to select a vintage that pairs best with a unique evening. Forgot cups? Just ask the usher.

Columbus Civic Theater
3837 Indianola Ave. in Clintonville, 614-447-7529
columbuscivic.org

TIP
In a parking lot south of the theater sits an unsuspecting yellow food truck. Go! La Poblanita serves mouthwatering, authentic tacos that will fill you up before the show. Another tip: bring cash. And the green sauce is spicy.

SPEND A HOLIDAY
AT THE ZOO

Every winter the world-renowned Columbus Zoo and Aquarium presents an incredible showcase made up of millions of twinkling LED lights. Starting in November, the myriad areas of the zoo, like Heart of Africa and Asia Quest, are expertly decorated with a magical multitude of twinkling holiday lights. Adored by children, Wildlights is also a favorite for adults. Don't be surprised if you see a proposal or two during a moonlight visit. Santa Claus and a few elf helpers make a stop every night to take down eager children's wish lists, and a dancing display of lights on the main entrance's pond set to holiday songs is a memory visitors won't soon forget. Bundle up, take a walk through the winter wonderland, and snack on some chestnuts roasted on, what else, an open fire.

Columbus Zoo and Aquarium
4850 W Powell Road, 614-645-3400
columbuszoo.org

TIP
The zoo is open every day of the year except Thanksgiving and Christmas, with extended hours for Wildlights, which is not lit on Christmas Eve.

STOP AND SMELL
THIRTEEN ACRES OF ROSES

More than twelve thousand roses of four hundred different varieties comprise the public Park of Roses in Clintonville. Located down the winding trail of Whetstone Park, the rose gardens are free to visit and open from dawn to dusk. In late May the Heritage Rose Garden blooms; stop by to see flora varieties that were grown as far back as the Roman Empire. Most of the roses reach peak bloom in mid-June, and the fragrant, colorful flowers last throughout the summer. By fall, the birds and other wildlife get their fill before heading south for the winter, which offers an equally unique view of nature's quiet but important slumber. The Park of Roses is located near a row of tennis courts, kids' playgrounds, and an entrance to the Olentangy Trail, so recreational activities abound following a peaceful walk through the flowers.

Park of Roses
Hollenback Road in Clintonville's Whetstone Park,
behind the library, 614-645-3391
parkofroses.org

GET TO
A GALLERY HOP

The first Saturday of every month marks the Short North Arts District's big night. This area of town, rife with art galleries, shopping, dining, and nightlife options, is nationally recognized as the best in the city. During Gallery Hop, the stores and galleries extend their hours so visitors can indulge in the culture and camaraderie for which this district is beloved. Come early to grab some grub at one of the many local restaurants—we love Philco Diner's Havarti, Ohio cheddar, and Nutella grilled cheese and root beer float for maximum art-viewing sustenance—then make your way to hotspots like Sherrie Gallerie, Brandt-Roberts, and Roy G. Biv to see classic and experimental work by artists from across the country. Street vendors and performers speckle the sidewalks, and most of the shops stay open until around 10 p.m. Afterward, try a pint from Short North Tavern, see a Nina and Virginia West family show at Axis or Union, or for dancing head to the Park Street complex just south of Goodale Park. Gallery Hop is unique each month, but a visit always guarantees a hangout amid the movers and shakers of the 614.

Throughout the Short North Arts District
shortnorth.org

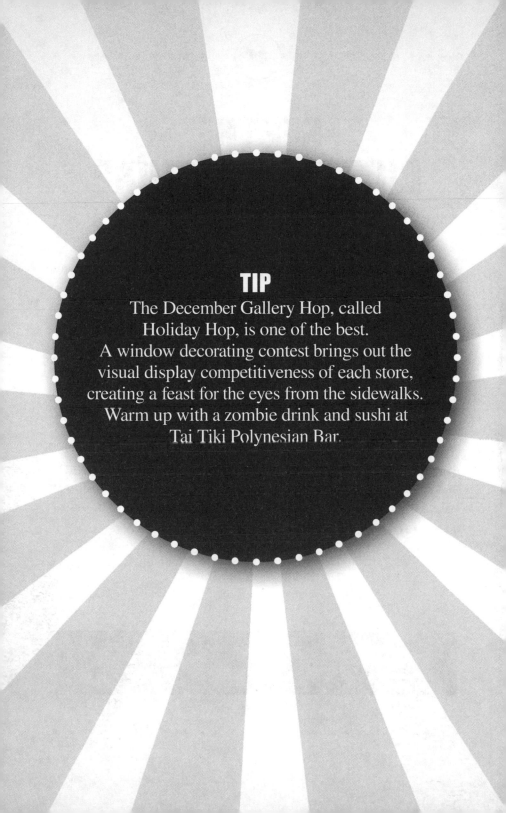

TIP

The December Gallery Hop, called
Holiday Hop, is one of the best.
A window decorating contest brings out the
visual display competitiveness of each store,
creating a feast for the eyes from the sidewalks.
Warm up with a zombie drink and sushi at
Tai Tiki Polynesian Bar.

SEE THE BUTTER SCULPTURE
AT THE OHIO STATE FAIR

Ah, the Ohio State Fair. Longstanding as the best place for people watching in the capital city, the fair is also a comprehensive display of the state's outstanding agriculture and animal science. All the classic fair standards are here—national entertainment like recent performers Aretha Franklin and Cheap Trick, equestrian competitions, and deep-fried Oreos—but an attraction that must be on every fairgoer's list is the butter sculpture. Each year a team of artisans molds thousands of pounds of the cold dairy foodstuff into lifelike, life-size statues of people, places, or things iconic to the Ohio landscape, which are then displayed in a forty-six-degree cooler in the Dairy Products Building. The 2015 display featured likenesses of Ohio State's championship-winning football coach Urban Meyer and mascot Brutus Buckeye. In a nod to the state's plethora of dairy farms and the animals that make the butter sculptures possible, there's always a butter cow. Don't be shy: take a churn (get it) up close to the glass for a pic.

Ohio Expo Center/Ohio State Fairgrounds
717 E 17th Ave., 614-644-3247
ohiostatefair.com

TIP
Don't forget cash for parking, typically around five dollars per car.

SEE A MASTER
AT THE COLUMBUS MUSEUM OF ART

The well-respected Columbus Museum of Art has a little something for every artistic taste. The collection features late nineteenth- and twentieth-century American and European modern art, including impressionism, German expressionism, and cubism, among others. Each genre has its own outstanding display at the museum, complemented by ever-changing main and sub-exhibits. View the woodcarvings by folk artist Elijah Pierce, who called Columbus home, as well as George Bellows, a fellow artist native to Ohio. Or gaze upon the recently acquired Photo League collection of works by American social photographers such as George Tooker, Rockwell Kent, and Lucile Blanch. There's a Wonder Room for children to play in and make their own masterpieces, while a recently added fifty-thousand-square-foot wing is the shiny new space for more permanent collection pieces, like Edward Hopper's *Morning Sun* when it's not traveling the country, and important exhibitions making a Columbus stop on their world tour. In the fall of 2015, the museum opened a new wing that gives it's stone facade architectural drama and even more viewing space for its 13,500 items. Admission to the galleries at the CMA is free on Sundays!

Columbus Museum of Art
480 E Broad St. east of the statehouse, 614-221-6801
columbusmuseum.org

TIP
Feeling artistically inspired? After a stop at the CMA, head a block west to the Columbus College of Art and Design's campus and snap a shot of the school's iconic red ART sign.

FEEL THE MAGIC
OF MOVIES UNDER THE MOONLIGHT

Watching movies outside on giant screens is a favorite summer pastime of the sunset-fun-seeking Columbusite. Pools, shopping centers, and village parks across the I-270 inner belt present a playbill of movies to be watched al fresco. Three favorites include the Wex Drive-In's indie hits and cult classics like *Cry-Baby* and pretty much the whole Wes Anderson canon. Screen on the Green in Goodale Park presents a pumped-up big screen on the green space's softball field, bringing hundreds to circle around on blankets and lawn chairs for a classic film and yummy snacks from food trucks. The North Market's family-friendly film fare offers a fun excursion to the Arena District.

Wex Drive-In
1871 N High St. in the Wexner Center promenade
wexarts.org

Screen on the Green
At Short North Goodale Park's southeast corner
goodalepark.org

Downtown Drive-In, North Market
59 Spruce Street
northmarket.com

TIP
The Ohio Theatre also has a classic Old Hollywood movie series throughout the summer. Parking beneath the statehouse is a best bet.

GET CONTEMPORARY
AT THE WEX

When the Wexner Center for the Arts, affectionately known as the Wex, opened in 1989 thanks to a major donation to Ohio State by Limited Brands founder and Columbus resident Les Wexner, the cultural topography of the state changed for good. The white metal grid architectural design led by Peter Eisenman is the visitor's first inclination of the contemporary art this institution displays and fosters. Regular gallery shows, film events, beloved indie bands and musicians, and experimental dance and theater performances welcome the best and brightest of the international art scene. Catch a lecture by visiting filmmakers and artists before viewing the latest exhibitions; there's always something happening at this standout incubator for creative experience.

Wexner Center for the Arts
1871 N High St. on Ohio State's campus, 614-292-3535
wexarts.org

TIP
Easy public parking can be found in the nearby Ohio State Student Union garage across the street from the Newport. Before you leave, though, head across the street and north a few blocks to eat a jelly donut at the diner-style bar of Buckeye Donuts—open twenty four hours for your taste buds' pleasure.

THROW SPOONS
AT THE BIG SCREEN

Yes, spoons! The Drexel movie theater in Bexley is a film fan favorite, bringing commercial, independent, and foreign titles to its locally run big screens. Among the events that have made it a staple are Casablanca Night, sci-fi marathons, Summer Kids Movie Fest, and Cult Movie Saturdays. That last one is when viewers can come and watch *The Room*, a 2003 drama that has gone down in the annals of cinematic history as the best worst movie ever. In the spirit of *Rocky Horror Picture Show* crowd interaction as the film rolls, *The Room* watchers participate in making this terribly acted movie even more fun—by throwing plastic spoons at the screen when the camera pans to the fake set's strange spoon-themed decor.

Other independent celebrations of film are available too. Head to Clintonville's Studio 35 to grab a beer at the lobby bar before catching a show. Or try the Gateway Film Center in the heart of High Street (if you park in the garage, the theater will validate your parking so bring your ticket inside). The Gateway posts all the current big box office hits as well as special one-off events that showcase classic old movies or experimental and foreign must-sees. The Gateway's Documentary Week is always a favorite, as are free showings of popular TV shows like *Mad Men* or the presidential debates, during which visitors often play drinking games with the theater's adult concessions.

Excellence in independent film and video artistry is celebrated during the six-day Columbus International Film + Video Festival held each November. Clocking in at more than sixty years old, this fest is the longest running one of its kind in the US.

The Drexel
2254 E Main St. in Bexley, 614-231-1050
drexel.net

Studio 35
3055 Indianola Ave., 614-261-1581
studio35.com

Gateway Film Center
1550 N High St, in the South Campus Gateway, 614-247-4433
gatewayfilmcenter.org

**Columbus International
Film + Video Festival**
columbusfilmcouncil.org

VISIT THE DRIVE-IN
AT NIGHT ... AND IN THE MORNING

A drive-in movie theater on the south end of town offers fun double features of new movies. For less than ten dollars admission on Fridays and Saturdays, visitors can watch from their cars, getting sound through an FM radio station. There's a concession stand with all the standards—hot dogs, cheese nachos, and candy—and grills are available until dark. After a night at the movies, head back to the drive-in Wednesday, Saturday, or Sunday for the Westland Flea Market. Vendors at this giant yard sale sell everything from old ham radios to classic car parts to antique jewelry. The flea is held from 5 a.m. to 1 p.m., mid-March to mid-November. The early bird gets the best trash-to-treasures.

South Drive-In Theater
3050 S High St., 614-491-6771
southdrive-in.com

PRACTICE YOUR PEACE SIGNS
AT COMFEST

ComFest is short for community festival, and this June weekend party has been a local favorite since 1972. Performers, food vendors, crafters, and social justice organizations provide the official entertainment at this free Goodale Park experience, and its reputation as a free-love, all-are-welcome celebration means the people watching is at a premium (one man's pet boa constrictor and women with painted breasts are famous at ComFest). The ComFest mission is to provide an outlet for social justice and politically liberal voices at various tents and stages as well as raise support for local programs with a community-building mindset. The beer booths and tents are popular, as this is typically the first big foray of summer drinking and sun bathing of the season. Buy a mug and some tokens, then find some shade and raise a glass to living "every day the ComFest way." Drink up: tips from beer sales go to local homeless shelters and other organizations.

ComFest
comfest.com
Held every June in Short North's Goodale Park

TIP
Off-Ramp Stage is where to find the up-and-coming new music of Columbus.

WATCH A BRAWL
AT THE ARTISTS WRESTLING LEAGUE

The traditions of art and the art of giant men in masks doing dropkicks in a ring collide at this recurring live event! Though there is no actual physical wrestling, the local artists, with wrestling-style personas, backstories, and outfits, talk smack and reveal a tall tale that would make the WWE proud. Nay, the battle takes place on the canvas as each wrestler makes live action art. Just hope the villain on hand doesn't slash the painting before it's done. Grab a seat at the designated battleground (typically 400 West Rich or the neighboring Vanderelli Room art gallery) and enjoy the high-octane art show. The rowdy nights are a great time to mingle among the city's most creative. Picasso 3:16!

400 West Rich
400 W Rich St. in Franklinton
facebook.com/ArtistsWrestlingLeague

Vanderelli Room
218 McDowell St. in Franklinton, 614-403-4689
thevanderelliroom.com

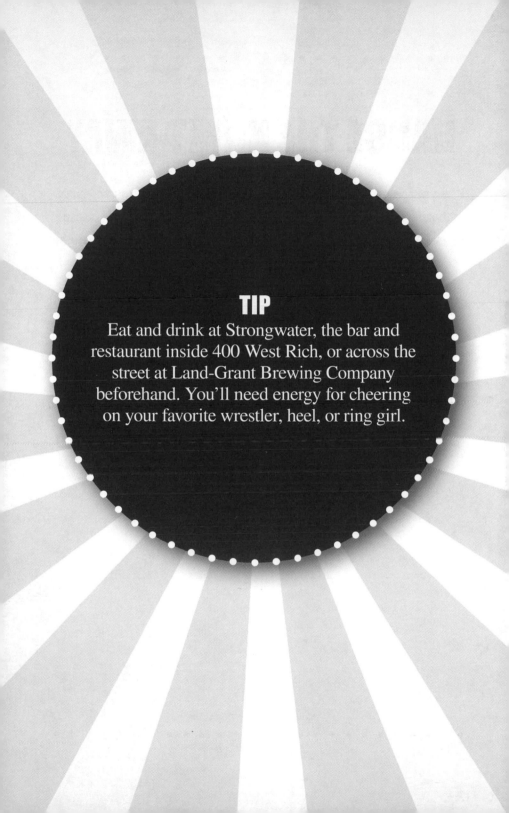

TIP

Eat and drink at Strongwater, the bar and restaurant inside 400 West Rich, or across the street at Land-Grant Brewing Company beforehand. You'll need energy for cheering on your favorite wrestler, heel, or ring girl.

DANCE THE NIGHT AWAY

Put your party shoes on and head to one of the many dance gatherings in town where local DJs spin the best of their chosen genre. Music video–worthing lighting and bars full of dance night specials abound. Damn Girl gets funky. Ogee brings the old-school hip hop, while Ladies 80s & More brings the Madonna and Prince. Heatwave makes things steamy with Motown, R&B, and old soul, while Swank shakes things up with vinyl from the '20s, '30s, and '40s. Dress codes for each dance party vary, so check the website or Facebook pages for details. Regardless of what you wear on the dance floor, prepare to sweat, prepare to move, and prepare to fall in love.

Damn Girl
Every third Friday at Strongwater Food & Spirits
401 W Town St. inside 400 West Rich in Franklinton
614-928-3170
strongwatercolumbus.com

Ogee
(dress code strictly enforced)
facebook.com/ogee.columbus

Heatwave
Every first Saturday from 9 p.m. to 2 a.m. at Ace of Cups
2619 N High St. in Clintonville, 614-262-6001
aceofcupsbar.com

Ladies '80s & More
Every Thursday at Skully's
1151 N High St. in the Short North, 614-291-8856
skullys.org

Swank
Every fourth Saturday at Short North Stage
1187 N High St. in the Short North
facebook.com/swankcolumbus

SEE A LIVE PRODUCTION
OF *THE NUTCRACKER*

Take part in an annual tradition that celebrates the spirit of the holiday season with song, dance, and everyone's favorite fairy tale. BalletMet is a professional troupe of dancers that travels the world performing. The dancers are led by renowned former New York City Ballet dancer and current BalletMet artistic director Edwaard Liang. Every year the company puts on a month-long production of Tchaikovsky's *The Nutcracker*, with the Columbus Symphony Orchestra playing the famous score from the pit. Both little ones and grown-ups with a childlike sense of wonder will enjoy the spectacle of an exquisite set and costumes, premier dancing, and stage acting. Join Clara on her adventure to a fantasy dreamland where sugar plum fairies and a handsome prince will pirouette into one of your family's best memories.

Ohio Theatre
39 E State St. downtown across from the statehouse on the south side
614-469-0939, capa.com

TIP
While enchantment is great and all, the kids will be hungry afterward. Try Chintz Room on High St. across the street from the Ohio Theatre block.

GET CLASSY
DOWN BY THE RIVER

Starring the city's outstanding performers, from bluegrass to circus acts to ballet, the Rhythm on the River series is a lovely way to spend an evening taking in the city skyline and enjoying some free entertainment. Performances take place at the Bicentennial Park Performing Arts Pavilion. This state-of-the-art stage faces stone stadium-style seating, giving viewers an unrivaled backdrop of the scenic Scioto River. Start saving seats around 6:30 p.m. and stock up on hometown hero Donatos pizza and water or beer. A slice of pie picnic with friends at dusk watching artists do what they do best? It doesn't get much better than that. If planning to cap a day spent downtown with a Rhythm on the River show, consider stopping in to two impressive art galleries that are also free. The Columbus Cultural Arts Center near the Milestone 229 restaurant has a monthly showcase of local and national art, while the OSU Urban Arts Space on Town Street, which is also within walking distance of the pavilion, displays thoughtful contemporary art exhibits.

Rhythm on the River
Throughout the summer at the Bicentennial Park Performing Arts Pavilion
South Civic Center Drive on the east side of COSI
sciotomile.com

SEE A BROADWAY SHOW
AT A HISTORIC THEATER

The fabulous Great White Way comes to Ohio during Broadway in Columbus productions. All the greatest hits like *The Sound of Music* and *Wicked* and modern must-sees like *The Book of Mormon* and *Kinky Boots* have made their way to the Ohio and Palace Theatre stages. These downtown venues feature unique historic architecture. The Spanish baroque style of the Ohio Theatre is an opulent setting for myriad musicals, while the subtle neoclassical vibes of the Palace offer a dreamy backdrop for the stars on stage (rumor has it that it's haunted!). Wine, soda, and snacks are for sale in the lobbies during intermission, lest hunger pangs get in the way of a fabulous sing-along. Season packages are available, which is the best way to get premier seating and exclusive presales.

Palace Theatre
34 W Broad St. (downtown), 614-469-9850
columbus.broadway.com

Ohio Theatre
55 E State St., across from the statehouse on the south side, 614-469-1045
columbus.broadway.com

INDULGE
IN BARBECUE AND BEATS

Everything is hot at the Jazz & Rib Fest: the music, the barbecue, and the weather. It's a recipe for lip-smacking good fun. Held in mid-July in the Arena District, stages at McFerson Commons and North Bank Park host live performances of outstanding regional and international jazz musicians, while a small jazz cafe resides at the North Bank Pavilion. Seating abounds and there are plenty of spots to find shade between sets. Amid the stages, of course, are the best boasters of barbecue ready to make your mouth water. Burners travel from ten different states and down from Canada to battle it out on the grill for the status of best ribs at the fest. Park on a side street in Harrison West, then follow the scent south to start taste-testing and declare your own winner.

Held in July downtown along the Arena District riverfront in McFerson
Commons and North Bank Park
hotribscooljazz.org

ROCK
ON THE RANGE

When the first Rock on the Range was held in 2007, big-name rock acts like ZZ Top, Velvet Revolver, and Breaking Benjamin headlining in one venue got national attention. It's only grown since then, and the fest of metal and mayhem draws visitors from every state and a noteworthy number of rockers from across the globe. Held in Mapfre Stadium, where Major League Soccer's Columbus Crew plays, Rock on the Range has a bunch of events on multiple stages in between the big-name acts with even bigger personalities (hello, Judas Priest). There's a competitive battle of local bands, a high-energy comedy tent, and an interactive graffiti art installation. Come for a sweaty mess and a raucous crowd, just like the rock gods intended.

Mapfre Stadium
1 Black and Gold Blvd. off I-71 North
rockontherange.com

WATCH A MUSICAL

Searching for some song and dance? Look no further than Shadowbox Live in the Brewery District. This nonprofit performance troupe writes, produces, and performs rock musicals in its top-notch theater. Get a gourmet pizza for the table (the actors are the servers) and sit back as a live band plays the musical numbers. Sometimes irreverent, always fun, these shows are an entertaining night out in the district. If there's not a main stage performance the night you're looking to go out, there's typically a performance of stand-up, storytelling, or improv comedy in the entrance area, called the Backstage Bistro, that's well worth the small cover.

The Short North Stage presents mainstream musicals and original productions as well as small theater and dance shows. The stage's resident dance troupe, Columbus Moving Company, explores social issues through dance in regular performances. Choreograph some time into the schedule beforehand to sit and sip at the beautiful wooden bar at the adjoining Ethel's Stage Left Lounge.

The Short North Stage
1187 N High St., 614-725-4042
shortnorthstage.org

Shadowbox Live
503 S Front St. in the Brewery District, 614-416-7625
shadowboxlive.org

SEE A BIG-NAME BAND
UNDER THE STARS

Lifestyle Communities Pavilion, affectionately referred to as the LC, is the nation's first indoor-outdoor concert venue. Rain or shine, the show goes on! The neighboring spaces are located in the Arena District next to Huntington Park's baseball diamond, so on evenings when there's a game and a concert, this part of town is hopping with energy. The outdoor stage is particularly exciting when the sun's shining. A sloping grassy hill provides ample seating for thousands and leads into a concrete-floored pit that gets fans close to the stars with guitars. There's not a bad seat in the house, which is why Top 40 bands and major tours drop in to the capital city to play here. The giant beer pours and Mikey's Late Night Slice in the pizza stand slinging pizzas by the slice to soak it all up finish off a summer night of singing as the sun sets.

Lifestyle Communities Pavilion
405 Neil Ave. next to Huntington Park, 614-461-5483
promowestlive.com

HEAR EVERY BEATLES SONG
EVER RECORDED PLAYED IN CHRONOLOGICAL ORDER

If ever a local music scene knew how to honor its heroes, it's this one. Columbus has a number of incredible cover bands, like Mr. Fahrenheit and the Loverboys, a raucous and theatrical take on Queen, or the Pinkertones, a group of music-playing Weezer fans that slays songs from the rock band's *Blue Album* and *Pinkerton* era. But the standout tribute is that of, what else, the Beatles. This twelve-hour behemoth of an event, usually held a few days after Christmas in a stained-glass-covered renovated church called the Bluestone, the Beatles marathon consists of 214 songs by the Fab Four played album by album in chronological order. The nonstop show welcomes many Columbus musicians to the stage and lively performance after performance. Hundreds of Beatles fans come to the family-friendly display of talent, as well as those impressed by the sheer musical and physical feat of re-creating such a massive amount of legendary work. Ladies and gentlemen, it's the best Beatles marathon this side of the big pond.

Beatles Marathon
facebook.com/beatlesmarathon

WATCH
A LOCAL ROCK SHOW

The grassroots support and music lovers of Columbus have bred all kinds of tonal talent. This is where bands like country superstars Rascal Flatts, two-piece phenomenon Twenty-One Pilots, and indie favorites Times New Viking and Saintseneca got their start. Despite the great variety of genres, rock is king here. Stages that welcome the smutty, sweaty, sexy scene that makes rock and roll the kind of thing that will never die abound in Columbus. A righteous underground sorta vibe thrives at many local shows and the bands that dominate metal, punk, experimental, and everything in between find homes at the following dimly lit stages throughout the entire week. Grab a bar stool and a cold one and prepare to forget the day the best kind of way.

Ace of Cups
2610 N High St. in Clintonville, 614-262-6001
aceofcupsbar.com

Spacebar
2590 N High St. in Clintonville, 614-784-0477
spacebarcolumbus.com

Skully's Music-Diner
1151 N High St. in the Short North, 614-291-8856
skullys.org

Carabar
115 Parsons Ave. in Olde Towne East, 614-223-1010

Little Rock
944 N Fourth St. in Italian Village, 614-824-5602
littlerockbar.net

Tree Bar
887 Chambers Road in Grandview, 614-725-0955
treebarcolumbus.com

ROCK OUT
AT THE NEWPORT

A stone's throw from OSU's campus, Newport Music Hall headlines big-name national music acts on tour. It's here that U2 played its first American show and John Lee Hooker played a final famous sendoff show before his death. Today, it's a cavernous, dive-y sort of joint with the grungy vibe that rock music lovers know and love well. There's plenty of room to watch the live show from the descended main floor or standing room that frames it, but the best seats in the house are upstairs. If the balcony is open, pop up there for carpet-covered, bleacher-style seating to kick back, have a beer, and enjoy the show.

Newport Music Hall
1722 N High St. across from the Ohio State Student Union
614-294-1659, promowestlive.com

TIP
Considering that it's on campus, options abound for imbibing some liquid courage before hitting the Newport pit. But if the popular picks nearby are full—which they will be many nights—search your smartphone for directions to Mama's Pasta and Brew. Just a few blocks away in a safe but secluded alleyway, Mama's is a watering hole dating back to 1977 that's got great deals on pitchers, plus billiards and darts.

TAKE THE RADIO
TO THE STAGE

In an era when big conglomerates rule the radio waves, Columbus's CD102.5 alternative independent radio station is like when you find that the hidden track on an album is the best song the band's ever played. CD102.5 is beloved for its long-standing reputation of bringing indie music hits to Columbus radio before any other station. Fittingly, it has its own annual summer concert that draws thousands to the outdoor LC stage. Held toward the end of July, when summer's ripe and the music sounds extra sweet, Summerfest's lineup always includes up-and-coming acts and big-name favorites. The 2015 show featured Saint Motel, Matt and Kim, Atlas Genius, Cake, and Weezer.

The twenty-five-year-old station recently opened its own Big Room Bar, named after the space in its recording studio where acts record intimate acoustic sets. Located in the same building where the 102.5 DJs work, Big Room Bar is a cozy restaurant with drinks where music fans can talk rock.

CD102.5's Big Room Bar
1036 S Front St., 614-221-9923
cd1025.com

HISTORY AND CULTURE

STAGE A NIGHT OUT

The Contemporary American Theatre Company, known as CATCO, is an Actors' Equity production company with a six-show season and a downtown stage in the Vern Riffe Center, which houses both government and art programs. The location is unique for its floor stage, surrounded on three sides by bleacher-style seating. It's an intimate setup that requires thoughtful staging, and CATCO's professional team does it well. The offerings include dance, contemporary theater, and musical performances, and an annual production of David Sedaris's *SantaLand Diaries* has become an irreverent Columbus holiday tradition of Santa-bag-sized proportions.

CATCO
77 S High St. on the second floor of the Riffe Center
614-461-0010, catcoistheatre.org

TIP

If an evening show is on the agenda,
consider heading downtown early for dinner
and a stop at the Riffe Gallery, housed in the
same building as CATCO's stage. The gallery is
operated by the Ohio Arts Council and exhibits free
shows of work by renowned and promising artists
who live or work in the state.
On weekdays, a locally loved diner downtown
called Jack's, tucked into an alleyway north
of the statehouse, is a kitschy must for a
snack of shakes and fries.

SHOW YOUR PRIDE

Let your rainbow and glitter flag fly at the annual festival and parade that celebrates the LGBTQ and allied community and its civil rights history. Presented by Stonewall Columbus, this fest is bursting at the seams with events and entertainment inside Goodale Park and at the nearby nightclubs. Watch a national music act onstage and dig into Columbus's long line of food trucks. The Saturday morning parade, which features local businesses, drag queens, and churches, always has an important grand marshal. Past presenters to cap off the weekend have included gay rights advocate and Star Trek alum George Takei and Jim Obergefell, the Ohio man whose landmark Supreme Court case made same-sex marriage legal.

Columbus Pride Festival and Parade
Held every June in the Short North and Goodale Park
columbuspride.org

TIP

The progressive Columbus queens community and its forebears have birthed a very successful family of drag queen and kings known as the Wests. Matriarchs Nina and Virginia West lead the charge throughout the day on stages in the park and are joined by their crew, including the popular king Jamz Dean, at Axis and Union bars just steps away from the park after sunset.

LEARN ABOUT RACE
IN COLUMBUS

The past, present, and future of the African American community in Columbus is the catalyst for educational exhibits and events at the King Arts Complex downtown. Its Martin Luther King Jr. Day celebration features empowering musical and theatrical performances, displays on the civil rights movement, interactive art activities, and a keynote speaker to honor the life and legacy of MLK. Throughout the year, the institution presents art displays in its Elijah Pierce Gallery. Named after the folk artist who earned a place in art history books with his woodcarvings that depict African and religious legends and the everyday life of Columbus's African Americans in the early 1900s, the gallery aspires to continue providing a visual voice for the ever-evolving civil rights movement and black culture.

The King Arts Complex
867 Mt. Vernon Ave., 614-645-5464
kingartscomplex.com

GET SPOOKED
AT THE STATEHOUSE

A town as historically relevant to the state's industrial, agricultural, and political landscape, Columbus is bound to have a ghost story— or a hundred. Various tour groups offer trips to the best of the best, like Booze Boos, a ridiculously fun visit to the scary depths of the city's oldest and most notorious bars. The Ohio Statehouse offers a family-friendly haunting too. Journey by oil lantern light through the Greek Revival building's limestone corridors as a tour guide tells tales of a routinely spotted mysterious weeping lady in gray and President Abraham Lincoln's ghost finishing a dance with a former Ohio governor's daughter. When tickets go on sale in early fall, they go as fast as a headless horseman across a bridge, so reserve a spot on the tour early.

Ohio Statehouse
1 Capitol Square in the heart of downtown, 614-752-9777
ohiostatehouse.org

TIP

Get dinner afterward at Ringside Cafe. This boxing-and-politics-themed historic tavern located down Pearl Alley (across from the statehouse on the north side) serves one of the best burgers and ghost stories in town.

ENTER
A COSTUME CONTEST

Celebrate Halloween at Columbus's biggest costume party, HighBall. The two-day event features a roundup of the stages presenting the best fashion designers in town and their intricate and exquisite costume designs. Part street party, part fashion show, HighBall attendees mingle on High Street, which is dotted with beer tents, electrifying live performances, and Dia de Los Muertos tributes. Wearing a crazy costume is encouraged; much of the fun is seeing everyone's clever cultural references and freaky fandom. From spooky standards to clever takes on current events, past favorites include group costumes of popular cereal characters like Franken Berry and Boo Berry and life-size Wi people. After this, you'll be convinced that Halloween is actually the most wonderful time of the year.

HighBall
Held every October at the intersection of the Short North
and the Arena District
highballcolumbus.org

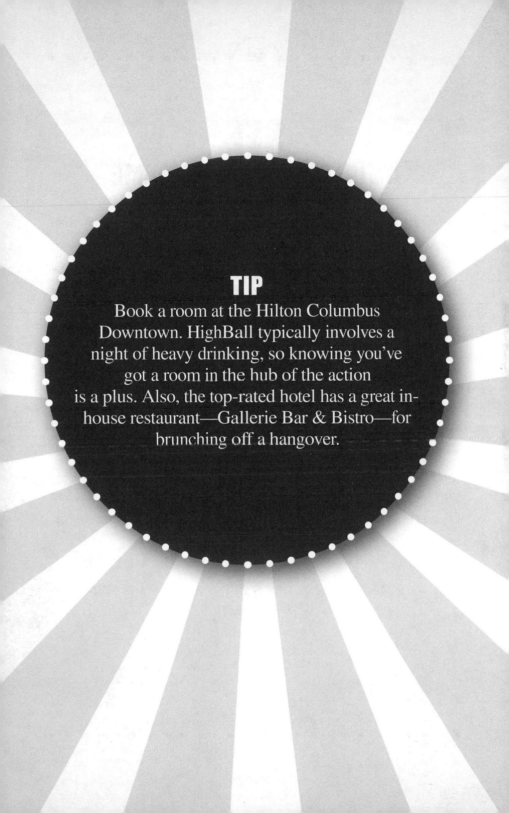

TIP

Book a room at the Hilton Columbus
Downtown. HighBall typically involves a
night of heavy drinking, so knowing you've
got a room in the hub of the action
is a plus. Also, the top-rated hotel has a great in-
house restaurant—Gallerie Bar & Bistro—for
brunching off a hangover.

SEE
A VINTAGE BASEBALL GAME

Travel back to the mid nineteenth century and watch teams of men dressed in buttoned-up shirts and pantaloons play a stripped-down version of America's favorite pasttime, following the same rules that were used when the game first got started. Called the Ohio Village Muffins, this team of bat swinging, baserunning re-enactors plays during the spring and summer at the Ohio History Connection's outdoor living museum called Ohio Village. A fun interactive visit to Ohio Village awaits in the fall and winter too. This sprawling re-created town is also home to the annual Country Living Fair, where Americana crafts are available for the picking, as well as Dickens of a Christmas, a candle lit exploration of holiday carols and old-time traditions. While you're there, check out the interesting artifacts on view at the Ohio History Connection's museum—from ancient Ohio artifacts to battle flags, a reimagined 1950s-era Lustron home, and a gallery of rotating exhibits

Ohio History Center
800 E 17th Ave. near the Ohio State Fairgrounds, 614-297-2300
ohiohistory.org

TOUR A VILLAGE
INSPIRED BY FRANK LLOYD WRIGHT

The organic design aesthetic of esteemed American architect Frank Lloyd Wright inspired an entire neighborhood of homes in Worthington. Building of the gorgeous unique structures began in 1956 and included a seven-hundred-foot triangular home. A drive through the scenic fifty-building-strong community is encouraged by the Usonian architectural landscape that blends privacy for homeowners with artistic facades for visitors. Flat roofs, natural lawns, sparse decor, and spacious overhangs denote the designs. Called Rush Creek Village, it's now listed on the National Register of Historic Places. Round out a visit with a stop at the nearby McConnell Arts Center of Worthington, which has displayed exhibits inspired by the historical neighborhood and regularly offers musical performances in addition to its visual art shows.

Rush Creek Village
614-885-1247, worthingtonhistory.org

PRETEND
YOU HAVE A GREEN THUMB

The horticultural institution on Broad Street called the Franklin Park Conservatory and Botanical Gardens is a sprawling campus of prolific plant gardens, indoor exotic plant displays, and rotating exhibits that display themed flora, fauna, and insects. The Blooms & Butterflies showcase held in the Pacific Island Water Garden starting in early spring is a colorful attraction, as is the winter wonderland of lights that lead to a darling display of poinsettia and other holiday foliage. Whatever time of year you come to walk through the permanent collection of warm gardens, it's an experience the whole family will enjoy. Don't forget the camera. A gorgeous backdrop for photographs, having a wedding here is a coveted experience. An expansive new building rendered from the repurposed wood of an Ohio barn acts as an educational lab for cooking, gardening, and horticulture classes. Check the website to sign up for a class, a Hot Shop glassblowing demonstration, or a guided tour of this lush nature landscape.

Franklin Park Conservatory and Botanical Gardens
1777 E Broad St., 614-715-8000
fpconservatory.org

TIP

The conservatory is open every day
from 10 a.m. to 5 p.m. and parking is free!
Don't miss the conservatory's farmers' market
on Wednesdays in October. Open from
3:30 to 6:20 p.m., the selection of fresh fruits
and veggies is complemented by
family-friendly entertainment and healthy
cooking demonstrations.

RIDE A HIGH-WIRE
UNICYCLE

Parents magazine named COSI, the Center of Science and Industry, the top science center in the country in 2008. Its renown is recognized by generations of Columbusites who have traveled to its downtown building on many a school field trip. COSI makes science fun with more than three hundred interactive exhibits that teach the foundations of discovery. Among the favorites is a high-wire unicycle ride. Test your balance and the nature of gravity on an eighty-four cable wire that's seventeen feet above the ground. Don't worry: a 250-pound counterweight maintains the one-wheeled machine's center of mass so the bike remains vertical at all times, and participants are hooked to wires and wear helmets. But COSI isn't just for kids! Host to traveling exhibits about everything from the *Titanic* to the human body, the science center also hosts monthly adult-only evenings out called COSI after Dark that include a lecture about a specific subject such as space or the science of sci-fi, suds from a local brewery, and a tour of the stars inside its state-of-the-art planetarium.

COSI
333 W Broad St. (downtown), 614-228-2674
cosi.org

TIP

There's public parking for a small fee on the west side of the building. Massive, rounded, and an impenetrable gray, the building was designed by famous Japanese architect Arata Isozaki.

GET LOST
IN A LITERARY ADVENTURE

Bookworms can burrow into the pages of a number of amazing worlds of words. Peruse the copious shelves and well-curated art gallery of downtown's diverse Columbus Metropolitan Library, the mainstay of the twenty-one-branch system that is routinely ranked as best in the country. Visit the Billy Ireland Cartoon Library & Museum, the world's largest academic collection of original comic strips and cartoon and graphic novel art that regularly displays its greatest hits. Tell a story at Wild Goose Creative's monthly Speak Easy event or attend one of this grassroots arts space's many pop cultural or comedic performances. Hear a visiting author read from his or her latest novel and discuss the art of writing at an Evenings with Authors event at Thurber House, the historic former home of humorist James Thurber. Round out the experience by stopping into Kafe Kerouac just north of Ohio State's campus. This cozy shop often has poetry readings happening on its small stage, while a bar and java counter sells concoctions named after literary heroes. Try the Roald Dahl—coffee with vanilla and peach.

Kafe Kerouac
2250 N High St., 614-299-2672
kafekerouac.com

Billy Ireland Cartoon Library & Museum
1813 N High St. by the Wexner Center, 614-292-0538
cartoons.osu.edu

Wild Goose Creative
2491 Summit St. by Rumba Cafe, 614-859-9453
wildgoosecreative.com

Thurber House
77 Jefferson Ave., 614-464-1032
thurberhouse.org

Columbus Metropolitan Library
96 S Grant Ave., 614-645-2275
columbuslibrary.org

SPORTS AND RECREATION

ROOT FOR THE HOME TEAM
WITH A HOT DOG

The monthly Dime-a-Dog Nights at Columbus Clippers baseball games are a local institution. Get as many hot dogs as your sunny-day appetite can handle for ten cents each while taking in the majestic seventy million dollar views of Huntington Park. It makes for a perfectly fun night out with friends, a date, or the kids—there's even a new playground located in front of the park to allow the little ones to let off steam during the seventh inning stretch. Grownups should take a walk around the park's spacious main deck to get a local brew and some grub from City Barbeque. But don't miss too much of the game. As the farm team for the American League's Cleveland Indians, the Clippers put on a great show and future baseball greats potentially dot the roster. Plus, the mid-inning mascot race is a chance to get rowdy in the stands. Go Lou Seal!

Huntington Park
330 Huntington Park Lane in the Arena District, 614-462-5250
huntingtonparkcolumbus.com

WALK AMID
A TOPIARY VERSION OF A FAMOUS FRENCH PAINTING

The painting *A Sunday Afternoon on the Island of La Grande Jatte* by Postimpressionist Georges Seurat is re-created out of life-size landscaped bushes and trees. This roundup of picnicking aristocrats and umbrella-hoisting society ladies tucked into the campus of Deaf School Park is called the Topiary Park. The imaginative scene is a relaxing oasis of greenery and dreaminess surrounded by downtown's bustle. The Topiary Park often plays host to outdoor summer movies and small community events. Also located on the seven-acre spot is a gentle pond meant to mimic the River Seine in the painting. The park is free to visit and open from sunrise to sunset. The best place to take a photograph is at the spot that designates where Seurat would have been standing if he were painting the topiary people out for a Sunday stroll.

The Topiary Park
480 East Town Street, Downtown, 614-645-0197
topiarypark.org

TIP
Check it out April through November for the greenest and fullest views of the landscape sculptures.

TAILGATE
AT AN OSU GAME

While one should obviously attend an Ohio State football game because nothing gets the adrenaline raging quite like the best damn band and football team in the land, it's the tailgating that's legendary. The lots surrounding Ohio Stadium are littered with fans of all ages starting as early as 6 a.m. on game day; try the lots west of State Route 315 to only be charged a few bucks for a spot. Make some new friends or hitch onto a buddy's RSVP to eat, drink, and be a Buckeye. Out-of-towners can park at the Expo Center, where the Ohio State Fair is held, and ride the COTA bus shuttle system back and forth. Don't feel like bellying up to a BYOB-style parking lot party? There are plenty of sports bars surrounding the stadium or on campus that will be a canvas of scarlet and gray. Try Little Bar or Eddie George's Grille 27. Wherever you are, remember that if a cheer of "O-H" is bellowed, the proper and only response is to shout back, "I-O"!

TIP

Traffic on and around campus during Buckeye home games is a nuthouse. Plan your travel accordingly. Those who avoid the gridiron? Game time is a great time to do non-OSU-related things in Columbus that might be too crowded for your liking on other Saturdays, like going to the Columbus Zoo and Aquarium.

CANOE
BIG DARBY CREEK

Do like Lewis and Clark and explore Columbus's wild side. Located in Grove City, a community just southwest of the I-270 inner belt, visitors will find Trapper John's, a canoe livery that has boats for boarding the Big Darby Creek, a tributary of the Scioto River. A trip up the waterway will reveal the state's impressive biological diversity (more than thirty-eight species of rare fish and mussels are reported to call this waterway home) and will provide a scenic calm from the hustle and bustle of the concrete jungle. Several itinerary options are available. A group can take a one- to two-hour trip downstream or spend a whole day (four to six hours) floating six miles on the preserve. Tubes are rentable if the weather's right, and for around twenty dollars per person a reservation-only guided moonlight tour is a serious memory maker. All rentals include access to a fifteen-foot canoe or kayak, paddles, and life jackets, and transportation to and from the livery.

Trapper John's Canoe Livery
7141 London Groveport Road in Grove City, 614-877-4321
trapperjohnscanoeing.com

TIP
Weather permitting, canoes and tubes can be rented on Saturdays and Sundays from 9 a.m. to 5 p.m. Pack bug spray, you tasty humans.

GO SLEDDING
AT HIGHBANKS

Ohio winters are notoriously unpredictable but snow is inevitable. Take advantage of the fluffy stuff and head to Highbanks, north of the I-270 inner belt. The 1,159-acre park offers a number of hiking trails of varying lengths, a nature center the kids will love, an eagle observation deck, gravestones of settling pioneers, and Native American–built earthwork mounds that are estimated to be more than a thousand years old. When it's time to sled, you'll want to head to the Big Meadows Picnic Area. Two sledding hills are here, including one that's perfect for kids under age ten. And although it's not in the park literature, Ohio snow is typically the perfect temperature and consistency for impeccably Instagram-able snowmen and snow angels.

Highbanks Metro Park
9466 US Route 23 North in Lewis Center
just north of the I-270 on-ramp, 614-846-9962
metroparks.net

ZIP-LINE
UNDER A FULL MOON

Fly through the sky at ZipZone in north Columbus at Camp Mary Orton. Reserve a spot for one of the several fully guided tours. A basic two-hour canopy tour sends you slinging from platform to platform over twenty acres of massive trees. The forest tour includes an education on the area's interesting wildlife and self-sustaining ecosystem. And a popular full moon tour happens when the moon is at its brightest; travel through the forest under the veil of dreamy darkness. During the week of Halloween, this tour takes things up a notch—zippers are encouraged to wear costumes, and a pumpkin-throwing contest is sure to induce the spooky spirit.

ZipZone Canopy Tours
7925 N High St. north of Worthington, 614-847-9477
zipzonetours.com

TIP
Spots fill up fast. Reserve a spot online beforehand.

CHEER ON
THE OHIO ROLLER GIRLS

The badass babes of the Columbus-based roller derby team play throughout the year at the Ohio Expo Center. The OHRG league, which has two teams, was one of the originals of the Women's Flat Track Derby Association and it now battles national and international opponents. In 2013 it earned its first world championship bid. Bottom line is these women are spectacular athletes, and as they make their way jamming, hitting, and gliding around the rink, spectators are destined for a good time and a good story. During timeouts, grab a beer and consider this: what would your roller derby name be—Ginger Snaps? Donald Pump? Discuss.

Ohio Roller Girls
ohiorollergirls.com

TIP
Want to do some skating? Hip hop and R&B night at Skate Zone 71 (unitedskates.com) is a weekly event that's got the tunes for making moves.

ICE SKATE
YEAR-ROUND

Still have *Frozen* fever? The Chiller ice rink has four locations—Easton, Dublin, Lewis Center, and the Arena District—that offer open skate experiences on well-kept layers of ice-cold fun. The NHL-sized rinks are guaranteed indoor excitement, and each has its own family skate packages and event schedule. Take a date to the eighteen-and-over night to show off your triple lutz or, more likely, ability to stay up on skates. For a cool family night, hit up Easton's Friday Night Meltdown, a teen-filled foray that heats things up with live DJs and disco lights. Check the daily rink schedule online. Rentable skates are available and a full concession stand provides extra energy.

OhioHealth Chiller Easton
3600 Chiller Lane by Easton Town Center, 614-475-7575
thechiller.com

OhioHealth Chiller Dublin
7001 Dublin Park Drive, 614-764-1000
thechiller.com

OhioHealth Chiller North
8144 Highfield Drive in Lewis Center, 740-549-0009
thechiller.com

OhioHealth Chiller Ice Haus
200 W Nationwide Blvd., 614-246-3380
thechiller.com

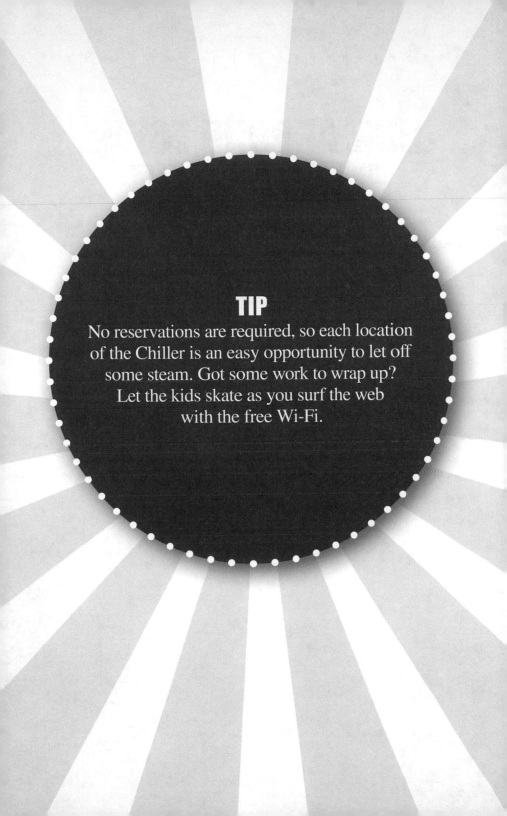

TIP

No reservations are required, so each location of the Chiller is an easy opportunity to let off some steam. Got some work to wrap up? Let the kids skate as you surf the web with the free Wi-Fi.

BIKE AROUND TOWN
ON BORROWED WHEELS

Take the Columbus streets on two wheels and borrow a bike from CoGo. This bicycle-share program instituted by the city of Columbus has bike racks throughout town that offer rentable transportation. Check out a bike, adjust it to fit your unique frame, ride it around, and then drop it off at the nearest docking station when you're done. Available to rent 24/7, and a twenty-four-hour pass costs less than $10; additional fees are incurred based on how long the bike is rented. Pedaling through the capital's myriad villages, parks, and trails is a healthy way to take in all its charm. The Olentangy Trail is a 13.75-mile journey of greenery- and goose-lined bike paths that is designed to take bikers from Worthington Hills to downtown with plenty of offshoots for a pit stop at a local pub, restaurant, or shop.

CoGo
cogobikeshare.com and check out the Station Map page
855-877-2646

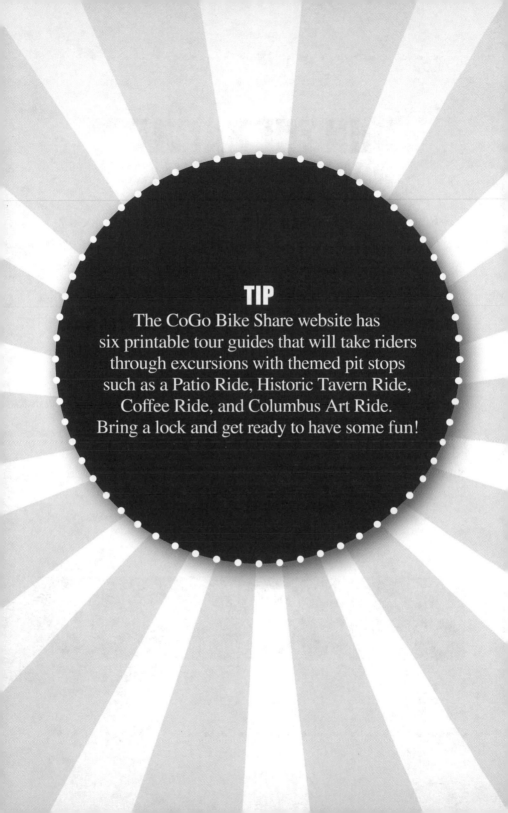

TIP

The CoGo Bike Share website has
six printable tour guides that will take riders
through excursions with themed pit stops
such as a Patio Ride, Historic Tavern Ride,
Coffee Ride, and Columbus Art Ride.
Bring a lock and get ready to have some fun!

JOIN THE BATTLE
WITH THE BLUE JACKETS

The Blue Jackets are Columbus's professional National Hockey League team. Despite their international fame, the Blue Jackets have a decidedly hometown appreciation. The team regularly raises money for local charities and the fans even got to name the mascot. Blue Jackets was the winner in a name-the-team contest and references Ohio's history as an essential part of winning the Civil War, honoring the soldiers who fought under this nickname. Today's ice-cold battle cry for the Blue Jacket brawlers can be heard from Nationwide Arena. The regular season runs from September through April, and these athletes—like rising NHL star Ryan Johansen and gobsmackingly good goaltender Sergei Bobrovsky—put on a brutal powerhouse of a show.

Nationwide Arena
200 W Nationwide Blvd. in the Arena District, 614-246-4625
bluejackets.nhl.com

TIP
Cheer like a local before the national anthem is sung by Leo Walsh. After the announcer introduces him, it's tradition for fans to bellow "LEO!" before "The Star Spangled Banner" starts.

BE A HOOLIGAN
IN THE NORDECKE

Considering that the nearly twenty-thousand-seater where the Columbus Crew plays was the first soccer-specific stadium built in the United States, it's safe to say that the heart of Ohio has heart for the game. In 2008, the team brought home Major League Soccer's greatest title, winning the MLS Cup, and the its legion of fans has only grown since then. The most dedicated of the fan base are called the Hudson Street Hooligans, and they regularly make huge pieces of art that taunt the opposing club or support their favorite players to display during the games. They pile into one corner of the stadium called the Nordecke, and every Crew fan should attend at least one game with the rowdy bunch's standing-only section. Or watch the match—and the Nordecke's playful shenanigans—from elsewhere in the stadium with some concessions from the southwest corner at Gate 6; here spectators will find local brews for sale, perfect for washing down Hot Chicken Takeover and Jeni's Splendid Ice Creams. The Crew obviously loves Columbus too.

Mapfre Stadium
1 Black and Gold Blvd. off I-71 North, 614-447-2739
columbuscrewsc.com
hudsonstreethooligans.com

RUN THE STREETS
OF DOWNTOWN COLUMBUS

Around fifteen thousand runners hit the pavement on High Street and the surrounding area for three races in early spring that comprise the high-energy OhioHealth Capital City Half Marathon. A half, quarter, and 5K run trek through Victorian Village, Ohio State's campus, and the wide streets of downtown, with a live concert and free champagne-fueled party at the finish line in the Columbus Commons. The impeccable views from these specially cordoned-off streets are topped only by the massive crowd of supporters and live entertainment stages that cheer runners onward. Want to walk? Go for it. This is the best tour of Columbus on two feet, however fast they move.

Capital City Half Marathon in June
capitalcityhalfmarathon.com

TIP
Runners and novice athletes can cross the famous Ohio State Buckeye's football field as well. The Ohio State Four Miler (ohiostatefourmiler.com) in October finishes on the famous fifty yard line.

GO ROCK CLIMBING
IN SCIOTO AUDUBON PARK

The Whittier Peninsula's 120-acre wildlife reserve belies its history as the city's industrial hub of factories, railroad yards, and metal warehouses. Today this lush area, located near the Brewery District, is an oasis of outdoor life, which visitors are more than welcome to get in on. Those looking for a nonparticipatory experience should stop into the impressive Grange Insurance Audubon Center to bird watch and learn about why this is a particularly tasty stopover for the birds as they migrate. The nearby Scioto Audubon Park is a city-lover-cum-outdoorsman's paradise. Start a day sailing the Scioto River from the boat ramp, hike the Scioto Greenway Trail, take the pup to play on the agility courses, or spike a game of sand volleyball on one of three competition-sized courts (BYOVB!). The most exciting feature, however, is the six hundred thousand dollar outdoor climbing wall, made of fiberglass and concrete. Pack up your ropes and equipment to start at the seven- or eight-foot boulders to warm up; then work your way to topping the thirty-five-foot tour to say you conquered the largest free outdoor climbing wall in the country. The park opens at 9 a.m. every day and closes at the same time as the park, which varies throughout the year. Plus, the wall's open until midnight the second Friday of the month, March through November.

395 W Whittier St. in the Brewery District, 614-891-0700
grange.audubon.org

GET IN THE CONVENTION CENTER
IF YOU WANT TO LIVE!

The first Arnold Classic, a multisport showcase of strength and talent, was first held in 1989. Since then the Arnold Schwarzenegger-hosted event has become an internationally prestigious competition and convention for athletes of all ages, disciplines, and skill levels. Offshoots of the festival take place in Europe and Brazil, but Columbus hosts the most elite of bodybuilding champions. Get pumped and spend a day perusing the long lineup of sports-themed vendors and watching everything from cheerleading competitions to male and female physique throw downs to bombastic table tennis battles. A sighting of the famous Austrian is likely also in the cards—Arnold visits his namesake festival every year to cheer on the competitors and hit up his favorite Columbus places like Mozart's bakery, crafter of authentic European pastries (it's diet cheat day, we assume).

Arnold Sports Festival held every March
Greater Columbus Convention Center
400 North High St. across from the Hilton
arnoldsportsfestival.com

TIP

The events for the festival take place around
Columbus, with the heavy lifting happening
at the convention center. For a guaranteed Arnie
photo op, head outside the center, where this
icon of the American Dream is commemorated
in an eight-foot bronze statue depicting
the Governator during his bodybuilding
glory days. Say protein shake!

TAKE A DANCE CLASS

Soar through the air in a former water fountain factory! The 400 West Rich building, a renovated warehouse and factory building in Franklinton that's an incubator for visual and performing arts, is home to Movement Activities. This troupe of aerial artists performs trapeze and silk stunts at the 400 Farmers Markets, Independents' Day, and other events throughout the year. The athletes present monthly workshops for beginners to the art of air to try out the sport. After participating in one of these classes, students can begin to attend weekly trapeze training, yoga, and bodybuilding classes to work their way to becoming a talented aerialist.

Contemporary dance laboratory Feverhead offers drop-in dance classes for adults. Learn a dance to a funky old jam or try your hands, legs, torso, and whatever else gets in on the free movement during an improv class at this proudly judgement-free zone.

And, of course, Columbus's premier professional troupe of ballerinas, BalletMet, has an academy that hosts weekly classes for adults in a range of genres and skill levels throughout the season. Dust off your dance shoes and train at the same barres as these graceful pros.

DANCE CLASSES

400 West Rich
400 W Rich St. in Franklinton, 614-360-3218
movementactivities.com
400westrich.com/art/classes/aerial-dance-classes/

Feverhead
1199 Goodale Blvd. in Grandview, 614-398-1198
feverhead.com

BalletMet Academy
322 Mount Vernon Ave. (downtown), 614-229-4860
balletmet.org

TRY A FREE
WORKOUT CLASS DOWNTOWN

May through September, free fitness classes perk up downtown's go-to green space, the Columbus Commons. The rectangular park, which is surrounded by office buildings, a historic theater, and beautiful condo and apartment buildings, hosts certified local professionals who teach yoga, zumba, boot camp, and interval training outside throughout the week, with the cityscape as aspirational inspiration. Before heading to class, register with the online waiver. It only takes a few minutes and registration will garner an all-access pass to the workouts throughout the season. Treat yourself to a carousel ride, a life-size game of chess to keep the competitive spirit up, or a visit to the Jeni's ice cream concession stand in the park afterward. Or stick around for an occasional free performance of a classic play by Actors' Theatre of Columbus. You earned it!

Columbus Commons
160 S High St. (downtown), 614-227-3788
columbuscommons.org

TIP

The Commons has inexpensive parking garages located beneath the park and across the street. The main garage entrance is at 55 E Rich St. and the underground entrance is at 191 S Third Street. The COTA bus system also has a drop-off at the south end of the park, so public transportation is another easy option.

SHOPPING AND FASHION

MIX A CUSTOM SCENT
AT THE CANDLE LAB

This local candle store has all the standard scents—rose, lemongrass, sugar cookie. But what makes it so beloved by its regulars and visitors alike are the novelty fragrances. Among them are bacon, amber musk, and buckeye, a chocolate-and-peanut-butter-smelling ode to Ohio's unofficial official confection. Head to one of its three locations (set up thoughtfully in neighborhoods noted for their stellar dining and shopping options) to either buy a single-scented candle off the shelf or blend a unique combination of three favorites. Here's how it works: customers sniff the store's 120 premade fragrances and write down their favorites. The pro-noses behind the counter act as guides as three are chosen. Decorate a label for the bottom, blend the oils until a covetable personal scent is absolutely nailed, pour the oils in the hot soy wax, and stir. The candles take about twenty minutes to make and an hour to set up (hence the well-planned locations), so hit up a neighboring restaurant or ice cream parlor during the wait. Nowhere else can one get a hand-blended candle that smells like, say, bacon chocolate apple orchard.

The Candle Lab
646 High St. in Worthington by Graeter's, 614-422-9900
751 North High St., 614-949-1458
thecandlelab.com

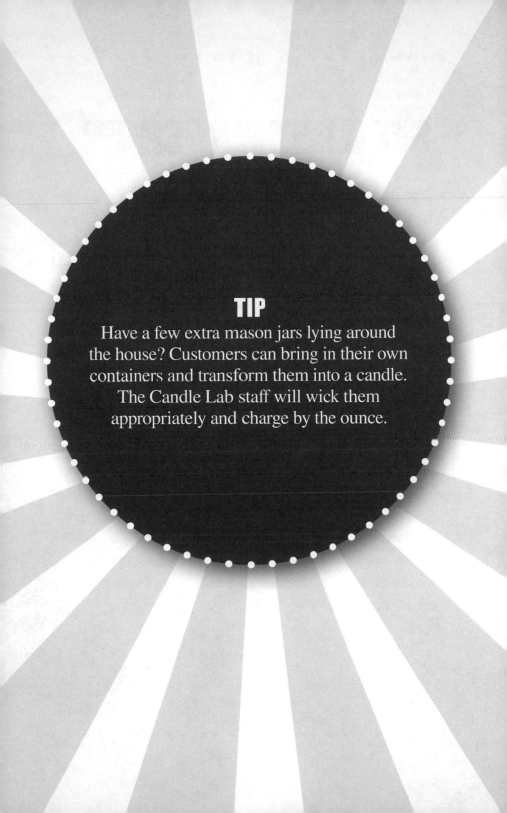

TIP

Have a few extra mason jars lying around the house? Customers can bring in their own containers and transform them into a candle. The Candle Lab staff will wick them appropriately and charge by the ounce.

SEE A RUNWAY SHOW

The Columbus nickname "Cowtown," reviled by locals, belies the capital city's status as an international hub for fashion. Central Ohio's Midwestern location, easy flight access, and diverse blend of people—and thus, diverse fashion tastes for testing—have made it a home for huge fashion brands. Victoria's Secret, Express, and Abercrombie & Fitch are all headquartered here. The talent pool of clothing designers is deep too, bolstered by two renowned Ohio fashion schools—Kent State and the Columbus College of Art and Design. The low cost of living in the state's major cities helps retain local talent, from fledging new grads to designers with national appeal, like Columbus-based *Project Runway* alum Kelli Martin. Martin co-produces an annual roundup of forward thinkers for the Alternative Fashion Mob. This runway production stars members of the coalition of Columbus's independent fashion designers; it's a veritable visual feast of punk rock attitude and avant-garde fashion, hair, and makeup. Once a year there's also Fashion Week Columbus. This high-end, multi-event sartorial showcase of Columbus designers culminates in a lush affair and a top-notch runway show, apropos of any fashion week.

Fashion Week Columbus
fashionweekcolumbus.com

Alternative Fashion Mob
alternativefashionmob.org

GET YOUR GIFTING
ON AT TIGERTREE

Regularly topping best boutique in Columbus lists, Tigertree is a husband-and-wife-owned store that's got a cute little something for everyone. Witty stationery, needlepoint mermaid flasks, edible chemistry kits, and gourmet sea salt soaps will top any gift-giving list. From ten dollar just-because presents to two hundred dollar clothing from popular indie designers like Ace & Jig, Tigertree is tops at curating a collection that's upscale with a sense of humor, and this is one of those shops where both men and women will find something new to obsess over. In late August 2015, the couple, inspired by their newborn, opened a children's clothing and toy store a few storefronts south on High Street cleverly called Cub Shrub. Shopping for someone who has the best-dressed baby on Instagram? Impress them with a gift from this charming new addition.

Tigertree
787 N High St. in the Short North, 614-299-2660
shoptigertree.com

LAUGH OUT LOUD
AT CRAFTIN' OUTLAWS

You know those craft fairs with doily art and sports team costumes for ceramic geese? Yeah, this isn't like that at all. Craftin' Outlaws is a biannual shopping event that showcases the best of Ohio and the surrounding area's alternative crafts. This includes items like crass cross stitch, vegan cookies, band art, grenade-shaped soaps, rum and coriander scented candles, and more. The vendors put a modern spin on traditional techniques, and supporting them at Craftin' Outlaws not only garners shoppers with a one-of-a-kind gift but also provides a chance to help small businesses grow. In addition to the fun shopping, visitors can get a taste of local beer or play a game to benefit a local charity. In the ten years since Craftin' Outlaws began, it has grown into one of the most anticipated, hippest shopping events in the city. The sprawling spring and fall events are held at various locations, but check the website to see if there are any roundups of the vendors at local events happening throughout the year. Hit any of them up for a craft that would make granny blush.

Craftin' Outlaws
craftinoutlaws.com

PICK LOCAL PRODUCE

Nurture the business of small, family-run agriculture at one of the city's many outdoor and indoor farmers' markets. Featuring the fruits, veggies, meats, and baked goods that were planted, born, or bred in the Buckeye state, these events are a delicious way to celebrate the Midwest's impressively vibrant farming community. At many of these farmers' markets, shoppers will find live music or entertainment from local artists as a backdrop to the fresh food air. The Worthington Farmers' Market also has an indoor food fair so shoppers can indulge in Ohio goodness year-round. Visit OhioProud.org for a list of current farmers' markets happening near you, and don't miss the following heavyweights of sidewalk horticulture.

Worthington Farmers' Market
worthingtonfarmersmarket.blogspot.com
8 a.m. to noon every Saturday, May-October
9 a.m. to noon Saturdays, November-April

Clintonville Farmers' Market
clintonvillefarmersmarket.org
9 a.m. to noon Saturdays, April-November
4–7 p.m. Wednesdays, July-September

North Market Farmers' Market
Starting at 8 a.m. summer Saturdays

WIN BIG
WITH A SPORTS TEE

When Homage started it was just a tiny T-shirt shop off a side street in the Short North. Since then it has become a major player in sports retail nationwide. What has made Homage such a big hitter? The brand offers a zany spin on culture and plays into the boisterous lifestyle of the most fun-loving sports fans. Cool designs that cheer on Ohio sports teams and cities as well as tees inspired by notorious subjects of music, video games, '80s wrestling, and more have made this laidback spot a shopping destination for anyone with a pop cultural pulse. Buy at least one tee: the staff stuffs into each bag a pack of old playing cards that idolize things like boy bands of the '90s or *Saved by the Bell*. You know, the important things in life.

Homage
783 N High St. in the Short North, 614-706-4254
4032 Easton Station at Easton Town Center, 614-532-5037
homage.com

ROCK OUT
WITH YOUR WALLET OUT

A pair of rock-and-roll-loving spouses own this must-visit shop in the Short North. Much of its devil-may-care merchandise is inspired by and features rock legends like Johnny Cash, the Sex Pistols, and Debbie Harry. From band logo baby onesies to skull and crossbones dresses for women to Sailor Jerry–style iPhone cases and handmade guitar pick jewelry, this store is jammed with trinkets, gadgets, and totems that hail to many a rock god. And, of course, they've got a killer playlist. What the Rock?! regularly showcases work by local artists, particularly those with a wonderfully creepy component, in its windows, so be sure to spend some time inspecting the spook.

What the Rock?!
1194 N High St., 614-294-9428
whattherock.com

MAKE A HOME
IN THE SHORT NORTH

The Short North is renowned as an arts district, but its shopping options are just as strong. Practically every retail spot on its High Street route has something for the home, from Anthropologie's quirky door knobs to the Lamp Shade's something-for-everyone selection of lighting. Get a new set of dishes designed to look like Pantone color cards or create a custom couch at Happy Go Lucky Home, which has a cute women's clothing store attached to it where they offer a variety of styles and sizes. Shop a bevy of odd beauties at Grandview Mercantile, which, even if you're not looking to purchase, is a museum-quality display of all things antique. Try Glean for quirky and cute decor that's made by local artists, designers, and crafters. For a full list of locations that are happy to help shoppers make a house a home, visit shortnorth.org/shopping/home-garden.

Happy Go Lucky Home, 962 N High St., 614-297-1100
happygoluckyhome.com

Grandview Mercantile, 873 N High St., 614-421-7000
grandviewmercantile.com

Glean, 815 North High St., 614-906-3178
shopglean.com

TIP

Many of the stores in the Short North are closed on Mondays. Having trouble finding a parking spot? Try the side streets west of High for safe and permit-free street parking.

DO MORE
WITH A CUP OF COFFEE

When a sales associate at Trek Bicycle Store in Upper Arlington offers you a cup of coffee, always say yes. It's fresher than you think! In fact, the shop has its own coffee microroasting business housed in a space behind the lineup of two wheelers. Aptly called Backroom Coffee Roasters, it's a great place to buy a bike and the quality beans that will fuel a future ride.

Try the new Roosevelt Coffeehouse downtown on East Long if making a difference is as high a priority as getting caffeinated. The brightly lit spot gives a portion of its sales to organizations that provide clean water resources for third world countries, educate poorer communities on how to grow their own food, and help provide a new life for victims of human trafficking. At Roosevelt, be sure to get for later a charmingly bottled java of Lokal, a Columbus business that sells Indonesian single-origin cold brew.

Just looking for a dang good cup of coffee so you can go do more? Stop into Yeah Me Too in Clintonville. The tiny blue exterior complements its cool no-nonsense interior that has little to no seating. Order a cup at the counter, pay, and head to the next locale.

Trek Bicycle Store/Backroom Coffee Roasters
1442 W Lane Ave., 614-486-8735

Roosevelt
300 E Long St. (downtown), 614-670-5228
rooseveltcoffee.org

Yeah Me Too
3005 Indianola Ave. in Clintonville near Savor Growl

STYLE A LOOK
OF DESIGNER THREADS

Columbus is a fashion-minded city and women's shopping options abound. Boutiques that offer everything from classic elegance to laid-back looks from the hottest independent fashion designers dot the city. Each has a unique ambiance with a fashion-editorial-worthy decor. In the Short North, neighbors Rowe and Ladybird have well-selected racks of contemporary shoes, accessories, dresses, and more. Stop into Rowe for pieces from Erin Kleinberg and bags by Foley & Corinna. Ladybird stocks Equipment, Zac Posen, and more. The editorial options continue at Thread, which has locations in Grandview and Dublin and offers pieces from exciting new designers and proven favorites such as Rag & Bone, Eric Clapton, and Maison Scotch. Leal in Upper Arlington is where to find more mature fashion options from designers like Alice and Olivia, Diane von Furstenberg, and Nicole Miller.

Thread
1285 Grandview Ave. in Grandview, 614-481-3090
shopthreadonline.com

13 S High St. in Dublin, 614-659-0800

Rowe Boutique
718 N High St. in the Short North, 614-299-7693
roweboutique.com

Ladybird
716 N High St. in the Short North, 614-298-8133
ladybirdfashion.com

Leal
2128 Arlington Ave. in Upper Arlington, 614-488-6400
lealboutique.com

LET YOUR INNER CHILD
OUT TO PLAY

Having fun in the Short North is bound to happen, whatever's on the itinerary, but three stores in particular are designed to take playtime to the next level. Stop into Big Fun—a favorite pit stop for nationally touring musicians and entertainers—to test fart machines and peruse classic old toys like Rock 'em Sock 'em Robots, My Little Ponies, and *X-Files* figurines. Looking for a gag gift? Big Fun has fake vomit options as well. Classic candy and soda pop is the theme of Rocket Fizz, a few blocks north. Pick up some Pocky sticks and IBC root beer then travel up the street to Rivet, a modern illustration and art gallery that sells quirky and highly sought-after designer toys certain to delight any cartoon lover.

Big Fun
672 N High St. in the Short North, 614-228-8697
bigfunbigfun.com

Rocket Fizz Soda Pop & Candy Shop
944 N High St. in the Short North, 614-525-0052
rocketfizz.com

Rivet
1200 N High St. in the Short North, 614-294-8697
rivetart.com

SECONDHAND SHOP
LIKE A PRO

Upcycling is a sport in Columbus, and many stores are renowned for their merchandise of pre-used decor, clothing, and oddities. Check out Rag-o-Rama in Clintonville to shop for gently used clothing for young men and women. The location balances name brand coolness with off-kilter clothing that's totally original. Midcentury modern and art deco artwork, bikes, furnishings, and music make up the Boomerang Room's collection. Make things mod with an old-school ottoman or bar set. Finally, Flower Child in the Short North is a destination any retro shopping fan should have on the to-do list. This cavernous space has room after room of stuff from the 1930s to the 1980s. Sunglasses, typewriters, clothing, vintage *Playboys*, and furniture are just some of the fun items up for grabs at this popular shop.

Rag-o-Rama
3301 N High St. in Clintonville, 614-261-7202
ragorama.com

Boomerang Room
3274 N High St. in Clintonville, 614-262-9661
boomerangroom.com

Flower Child
989 N High St. in the Short North, 614-297-8006
flowerchildvintage.com

GET IN ON
GIFT SHOP GOODNESS

The myriad tourist attractions in Ohio's capital city are also where to find some of the quirkiest shopping. Pick up Ohio-made and Ohio-themed items at the statehouse after visiting the spectacular rotunda of the people's house. Stuff a bag with Ohio-shaped cutting boards, historical cookbooks, and fresh maple syrup to remember a visit. The Wexner Center Store will appeal to gadget lovers and modern art fans alike, while the Columbus Museum of Art gift shop has items that relate to current exhibitions, and the staff offers free gift wrapping during the holidays. Shop literary mugs and clothing at the Library Store, garden essentials at the Franklin Park Conservatory, or Columbus's favorites and Ohio-made treats at the gift shop in the visitors center in the Arena District.

GIFT SHOPS

Ohio Statehouse Museum Shop
Inside the Ohio State Capitol, 614-728-9234
statehouseshop.com

Wexner Center Store
1871 N High St. on the OSU campus, 614-292-3535
wexarts.org

Library Store
96 S Grant Avenue on the first floor of the
Columbus Metropolitan Library
614-645-2275, columbuslibrary.org

Columbus Museum of Art
480 E Broad St., just east of downtown, 614-221-4848
columbusmuseum.org

Franklin Park Conservatory
1777 E Broad St., 614-715-8000
fpconservatory.org

Experience Columbus
277 W Nationwide Blvd., No. 125, 614-221-6623
experiencecolumbus.com

DO IT ALL
IN ONE TWO-BLOCK RADIUS

The South Campus Gateway is located on High Street just south of Ohio State's campus. Designed to be a hotspot for students off-campus and their visiting parents, it's buzzing with shopping, dining, drinking, and film entertainment. A two-story Barnes and Noble is near a cool and moderately priced women's clothing store called Pitaya. Go to Simply Vague, tucked into the south end's landscaped promenade, to shop more than thirty-five vendors who live and work in Ohio. Packed with artisanal food, funky home goods, and Columbus-themed apparel, this is the spot to get your Ohio love on before heading to happy hour and a movie. Speaking of the big screen, drop into the Gateway Film Center to see and purchase movie-themed art at the beloved theater.

South Campus Gateway on High St.
between campus and the Short North
southcampusgateway.com

TIP
There's a public parking garage behind the Gateway Film Center. If heading in to watch a movie, bring your parking ticket with you to have it validated so it only costs a dollar to exit.

BLEND A CUSTOM
COLOR PALETTE

An upscale spa in the Short North is where to go for a makeover or a stash of cosmetics blended specifically for your skin tone. This decade-old spot nails the art of Zen beauty and fragrance. Set up an appointment beforehand to have an expert colorist create recipes of two creams and powders, six eye shadows, two blushes and bronzers, six lipsticks, and Mukha mascara that look best on you. The cosmetics' ingredients are all free of oil, drying alcohol, or artificial dyes or preservatives, and they'll keep customers' specific recipes on file so they can easily re-order. Just want a massage? Who doesn't! The cushy spot has a list of relaxation services certain to make customers say, "Ahh . . ."

Mukha Cosmetics and Medi-Spa
980 N High St. in the Short North, 614-294-7546
mukhaspa.com

SPEND THE DAY
AT MORE THAN A MALL

The biggest shopping locales in Columbus are Easton Town Center and Polaris Fashion Place. Both have indoor, multilevel shopping malls and outdoor enclaves lined with international favorites.

Easton Town Center is a short distance off I-270 East close to Gahanna. Here, visitors will find more than two hundred stores, a variety of restaurants, a thirty-screen theater, comedy club, and game spot. Premier retailers include True Religion, American Girl, Madewell, Apple, and West Elm. Columbus makers hold their own too at Celebrate Local, which sells wares from more than three hundred Ohio artisans. Plan to spend a day shopping before dinner at Smith & Wollensky steakhouse or Brio Tuscan Grille, then see a show at the Funny Bone or catch a movie at the AMC theater. Nearby on the Easton Gateway are even more shopping options like Nordstrom Rack and Dick's Sporting Goods.

Polaris is north of I-270 and west of I-71. The two-level mall is home to standouts like Victoria's Secret, Saks Fifth Avenue, Macy's, and Banana Republic. An outdoor plaza offers ample seating for sunning between shopping and leads into a bevy of good food stops like Cantina Laredo (the guacamole made table side is a must!) and the Cheesecake Factory.

Easton Town Center
160 Easton Station, 614-337-2200
eastontowncenter.com

Polaris Fashion Place
1500 Polaris Parkway, 614-846-1500
polarisfashionplace.com

GET CRAFTY
IN CLINTONVILLE

It doesn't get much more adorable than Wholly Craft! Its pink facade beckons from High Street, and inside shoppers will find jewelry, baby clothes and toys, funny kitten tees, and handmade home goods from more than two hundred crafters and artists. From cupcake-shaped bath bombs to Ohio aprons with handy beer-holding pockets, Wholly Craft! is a favorite for a completely original, smart gift. It's consistently voted one of the best stores in Columbus and its owner is beloved for being the fun-loving fairy godmother of the city's vibrant craft scene. Do more than shop during a visit! The store offers many workshops and classes for kids and adults alike to learn how to do things like use a sewing machine or concoct their own cat-themed craft. Yes, a cat-themed craft. It's purrfect.

Wholly Craft!
3515 N High St., 614-447-3445
whollycraft.com

VISIT BIBLIOPHILE
PARADISE

Thirty-two rooms of books. Thirty-two! The searching reader need look no further for book heaven than German Village. Sectioned by theme, grab a tome or two and have a seat. This is the type of spot where getting lost in books isn't just a metaphor. Sports, cookbooks, fiction, literature, biographies, children's tales, LGBT erotica, etc. It's all here. Be sure to flip through the sales on the front patio too. A deeply discounted treasure typically awaits on the outdoor tables. National authors also love this shop; check out the online calendar to see if a favorite writer will be making the rounds of the thirty-two rooms and doing a signing and reading.

The Book Loft
631 S Third St. in German Village, 614-464-1774
bookloft.com

TIP
There's a Starbucks across the street if you want to get reading immediately, or in the summer head a few blocks south to read in the gorgeous Schiller Park before watching a live Shakespearean play.

MAKE YOUR OWN BOOK

A quaint street in the family-filled suburb of Worthington is where shoppers will find Igloo Letterpress, a letterpress and bookbinding shop that takes classic printing techniques and gives them a modern spin. Funny pop cultural references and whimsical designs decorate their store's cards, stationery, and posters. Looking for wrapping paper to wrap new purchases from nearby stores? Stop in to find an original print that balances cutesy charm with fine art. The skilled owner and team teach classes throughout the year in their industrious workshop where participants can create their own works of art with antique wood and lead type, bind their own books or journals, pen gold foil notecards, and more.

Igloo Letterpress
39 W New England Ave. in Worthington, 614-787-5528
iglooletterpress.com

TIP
During a visit, walk over to Sassafras Bakery for milk and cookie happy hour! Weekdays from 3 to 5 p.m., purchase a cookie and get a free glass of milk or cup of coffee.

SHOP STREET VENDORS
FOR UNIQUE ITEMS

Taking a note from the farmers' market playbook, local markets have started popping up that sell not fresh produce but all other kinds of goodies.

Columbus Flea is a popular recurring pop-up outdoor market that features a multitude of tables selling records, art, vintage clothing, zines, books, and handmade jewelry. A DJ spins while visitors sift through the finds, as resident restaurants, coffee shops, and food trucks keep everyone satiated for maximum shopping potential.

The Moonlight Marketplace on Gay Street aims to bring shopping back to downtown, long a habitat to mostly restaurants, businesses, and, of course, the statehouse. Starting around dusk, eager shoppers come in from the surrounding area to taste-test food from area restaurants and shop a mix of artisan vendors (like men's goods and stationery brand Robert Mason Co.) and booths by visiting brick-and-mortar stores. It's a sidewalk shopping experience that takes full advantage of the season's golden hour and then some. Street performers and painters round out the atmosphere of a feel-good evening out.

Columbus Flea
columbusflea.wordpress.com
Four seasonal fleas are held every year, dates vary per year.

Moonlight Marketplace
moonlightmarketcolumbus.com
6–11 p.m. second Saturday of the month, April-October,
on Gay St. downtown

TIP

Following a trek or two around the Moonlight
Market, check out the Columbus Commons for
live outdoor entertainment or the nearby
Tip Top restaurant for casual bar food
and its famous sweet potato fries.

MAKE A SHOPPING CRAWL
IN DOWNTOWN POWELL

The Powell community has a sleepy outsider charm with a lively-for-the-burbs downtown. Its main intersection of streets is dotted with elegant shops worthy of an afternoon excursion to this northwest suburb. Bungalow Home is in a renovated church with a modern Americana style. Find brilliant furniture made of reclaimed wood, iron chandeliers, or a chic necklace. Nicole's for Children showcases the best of baby apparel, religious gifts, and toys, while numerous antique and jewelry boutiques, like Liberty Antique Mall and Krysty Designs Fine Jewelry, round out the Powell shopping experience. Plan on settling in for dinner or a glass of wine after all that purchasing. Powell offers several fine dining options within walking distance of the shopping district. Taste a flight of Ohio wines at Powell Village Winery and dig into glazed Ohio scallops at Kraft House No. 5.

Downtown Powell
44 N Liberty Street
heartofpowell.org/shopping.html

ITINERARIES
BY ACTIVITY

FREE ACTIVITIES

SPORTS

DATE NIGHT

BEER

OFF THE BEATEN PATH

KID FRIENDLY

COLUMBUS CLASSICS

ACTIVITIES
BY SEASON

Ohio weather is predictably unpredictable. A summer day could bring fall temperatures and vice versa. Be certain it will snow in winter and rain in spring—and maybe hail in summer. Ask any Columbusite how to layer for the sudden changes (we're pros!) and try one of these activities you can predict on enjoying during each season.

WINTER

Ice Skate at the Chiller, 96

Wildlights at the Columbus Zoo and Aquarium, 38

Craftin' Outlaws, 116

Columbus Blue Jackets, 100

Beatles Marathon, 63

Kihachi, 22

Brewery tours, 30

The Nutcracker by BalletMet, 56

Sledding at Highbanks, 93

SPRING

Park of Roses, 24

Katalina's pancake balls, 15

Dime-a-Dog Night at Huntington Park, 88

Columbus Arts Festival, 34

Capital City Hall Marathon, 102

The LC outdoor concerts, 62

CoGo bike rides/ Olentangy Bike Trail, 98

Columbus Pride Festival and Parade, 72

ComFest, 49

SUMMER

FALL

INDEX

• •

• •